SCAR ON THE STONE

*Ova je knjiga posvećena
nestalima Bosne
sa nadom
da će biti pronadjeni
živi ili ne*

This book is dedicated
to the missing of Bosnia
in the hope
that many will be found
living or dead

scar
ON THE
stone

CONTEMPORARY
POETRY FROM
BOSNIA

edited by
CHRIS AGEE

BLOODAXE BOOKS

Translation consultant: Francis R. Jones
Literal translations: Antonela Glavinić and Igor Klikovac

ISBN: 1 85224 415 1

First published 1998 by
Bloodaxe Books Ltd,
P.O. Box 1SN,
Newcastle upon Tyne NE99 1SN.

Bloodaxe Books Ltd acknowledges
the financial assistance of Northern Arts.

ACKNOWLEDGEMENT

Acknowledgements and thanks are due to
the Soros Foundation's Open Fund Bosnia-Herzegovina
for assisting with the publication of this book
with a grant for the translators.

Cover printing by J. Thomson Colour Printers Ltd, Glasgow.

Printed in Great Britain by
Cromwell Press Ltd, Trowbridge, Wiltshire.

PG-A hierarchy of needs is built into the very fabric of reality and is
1417 revealed when a misfortune touches a human collective, whether
B6 that be war, the rule of terror, or natural catastrophe. Then to satisfy
53 hunger is more important that finding food that suits one's taste; the
1998simplest act of human kindness toward a fellow human being acquires
more importance than any refinement of mind. The fate of a city, of
a country, becomes the centre of everyone's attention, and there is a
sudden drop in the number of suicides because of disappointed love
or psychological problems. A great simplification of everything occurs,
and an individual asks himself why he took to heart matters that now
seem to have no weight. And, evidently, people's attitude toward the
language also changes. It recovers its simplest function and is again
an instrument of serving a purpose; no one doubts that language
must name reality, which exists objectively, massive, tangible, and
terrifying in its concreteness...

All reality is hierarchical simply because human needs and the dan-
gers threatening people are arranged on a scale. No easy agreement
can be reached as to what should occupy first place. It is not always
bread; often it is the word. And death is not always the greatest men-
ace; often slavery is. Nevertheless, anyone who accepts the existence
of such a scale behaves differently from someone who denies it. The
poetic act changes with the amount of background reality embraced
by the poet's consciousness. In our century that background is, in my
opinion, related to the fragility of those things we call civilisation
or culture. What surrounds us, here and now, is not guaranteed. It
could just as well not exist...

CZESŁAW MIŁOSZ,
The Witness of Poetry

Blue River

Where it might flow we do not know
not much is known except for this

beyond the hills beyond the vales
beyond the seven and the eight

from mad to mad from bad to bad
beyond the dour beyond the sour

and through the haws and through the thorns
and through the fires and through the pliers

beyond our wit beyond our sense
beyond all nines beyond all tens

from depth to depth from strength to strength
beyond the silent and the night

to where the horn's call no one knows
to where the cockerel never crows

from bad to bad from mad to mad
beyond our thoughts beyond our god

that's where the dark blue river flows
a river that is wide and deep

it is a hundred winters wide   •
it is a thousand summers deep

and of its depths don't even dream
its doom and gloom will never heal

that's where the dark blue river flows

that's where the dark blue river flows
this river that we have to cross

MAK DIZDAR (1917-71)
translated by Francis R. Jones

Black

(on the fall of Srebrenica, 11 July 1995)

A black day, this.
The sky is black.
The sea is black.
The gardens are black.

The trees are black.
The hills are black.
The buses are black.
The cars bringing the kids to school are black.

The shops are black.
Their windows are black.
The streets are black (and I don't mean with people).
The newspapers sold by the dark girl with the great head of dark hair
are black, black, black.

The ox is black.
The hound is black.
The very horse from Iveragh is black.
The bird suddenly out of sync with the flock is black.

The black sheep that stood out from the ordinary run of sheep
        no longer stands out, for all the sheep are black.

The spuds are black.
The turnips are black.
Every last leaf of cabbage in the pot is black.

The saucepan is black.
The kettle is black.
The bottom of every pot from here to the crack of doom is black.

The Catholics are black.
The Protestants are black.
The Serbs and the Croatians are black.
Every tribe on the face of the earth this blackest of black mornings black.

The politicians are scuffling about
biting the legs and the tails off each other
trying to persuade us
to look on the bright side.

Anyone who might be inclined
to take them at their word
would do well, maybe, to ask
why they think it goes without saying
that every black cloud has a silver lining.

I myself won't be the one.
For I'm black.
My heart is black and my mind is black.
Everything that falls into my field of vision is black.
I'm full of black rage.
There's a black mark against all your names.

Like each and every lump of coal, every blackberry and sloe
and demon and devil and Devil's Coachman,
every grave and cave and arsehole,
every bottomless pit in which we lose all hope,
I'm black as black can be.

Now that Srebrenica, that silver city –
Argentaria, as the Romans called it –
is blank.

NUALA NÍ DHOMHNAILL
translated from the Irish by Paul Muldoon

CONTENTS

ACKNOWLEDGEMENTS

I wish to express my especial gratitude to the following individuals who generously gave of their time and whose labours proved indispensable: Francis R. Jones, Antonela Glavinić, Igor Klikovac and Dženana Trbić of the Soros Foundation (Sarajevo). For a range of advice and assistance, my heartfelt thanks to the following: Angus Calder, Aida Čengić and Jakob Finci of the Soros Foundation (Sarajevo), Vojka Djikić, John Fairleigh of Queen's University (Belfast), Celia Hawksworth of the School of Slavonic Studies (London), Zdenko Lesić of Hankuk University (Seoul), Branka Magaš, Sonja Mehmedinović, Geraldine Mitchell, Majo Topolovac, Bill Tribe and Marko Vešović. I would also like to thank Bernard and Mary Loughlin of the Tyrone Guthrie Centre at Annaghmakerrig, Co. Monaghan, where some of my work on the anthology was done.

Acknowledgements are due to the following publishers. To Harper Collins Publishers Inc for the three extracts from *The Tenth Circle of Hell: A Memoir of Life in the Death Camps of Bosnia* by Rezak Hukanović (Basic Books, 1996). To Harvard University Press for the two extracts from *The Witness of Poetry* by Czesław Miłosz, copyright © 1983 by the President and Fellows of Harvard College. To Lilliput Press for the extract from *Mr Pfeffer of Sarajevo* (1956) by Hubert Butler, reprinted from his essay collection *Escape from the Anthill* (Lilliput Press, Dublin, 1985) by kind permission of Antony Farrell. To Penguin Books Ltd for the three extracts from *Sarajevo Marlboro* by Miljenko Jergović, translated by Stela Tomašević (Penguin Books, 1997, first published in Croatia as *Sarajevski Marlboro* by Durieux, 1994), copyright © Durieux, 1994; translation copyright © Stela Tomašević, 1997.

Thanks are also due to the original authors for allowing translations of their work to be published in this anthology. Every effort has been made to trace copyright holders of material included in this book. The editor and publisher apologise if any material has been included without permission or without the appropriate acknowledgement, and would be glad to be told of anyone who has not been consulted.

INTRODUCTION

This anthology emerged from a visit I made to Sarajevo in the spring of 1996. It was my first time in the city (the war had just ended), and although I was there only for seven days, it seemed much longer. Profound, moving, unforgettable, it was one of the most significant and happy moments of my life, in ways I still find difficult to unravel. It has since seemed a touchstone for the elasticity of time – for how things can slow into deeper experience when the habit of the daily is less firmly in the saddle.

That week, life seemed to jibe with a bracing wind from the republic of conscience. The city, dazed and weary after a siege as long as Leningrad's, was basking in the first light of freedom after the long tunnel of war and genocide. Its alpine beauty backdropped every chance encounter or conversation or vista with a landscape of ruin and suffering. Peace had not lost its shine, and the feeling of exhilaration was as palpable as it was contagious. You felt an effect of inward "cleansing", of clarifications on many fronts, as if the very harrowing of life by destruction had separated the essential from the chaff. Everywhere you looked you saw depth, tempering the patinas of routine and social surface, loosening the props which conveniently thwart our gaze into each *other*. Or instead of *depth*, should I say *death*?

I had stepped briefly, anyhow, into liberation – the rare historical moment where a window is flung open on two overlapping orders of time, war and peace, the inhuman and the civilised; and light is thrown on the strangeness of their simultaneity in the world at large. Later I would recognise something of what I had felt, in the city and in myself, in two comments I came upon in the ensuing months.

The first is something Samuel Beckett said of his time working with the Red Cross in Normandy in the immediate aftermath of the Second World War: 'Some of those who were in Saint-Lô will come home realising they got at least as good as they gave, that they got indeed what they could hardly give, a vision and sense of a time-honoured conception of humanity in ruins, and perhaps even an inkling of the terms in which our condition is to be thought again.' The other is by the Irish essayist Hubert Butler, who spent much of the thirties in Leningrad, Zagreb and Vienna. Speaking of his time with Quaker relief after the Anschluss, he wrote in 1988:

> I believe one of the happiest times of my life was when I was working for the Austrian Jews in Vienna in 1938-39. It is strange to be happy when others are miserable, but all the people at the Freundeszentrum in the Singerstrasse were cheerful too. The reason is surely that we have always known of the immense unhappiness that all humanity has to suffer. We read of it in the newspapers and hear it on the radio but can do nothing about it.

What I encountered in Sarajevo was not only a glimpse of humanity in ruins but an inkling of how certain things might be rethought. What I found in myself was the strange lightening that descends when the gap between the daily and the ethical narrows, when the ego faces windward towards that frugal republic. In short, something of the two great liberations: the one from injustice, the other from self.

All this is another way of saying I had tasted the joy of reconstruction. When humanity lies in ruins, when the house of light must be rebuilt, no task is surplus. The poem no less than the nail responds to the moral imperative of reparation. When, therefore, it was suggested in Sarajevo that I undertake two literary projects – one of them this anthology – my delight was tempered by a sense that it was not only a duty but a gift. Even an anthology published a thousand miles away might serve the rising house of light by lifting the curtain on both the polyphony that was prewar Bosnia and the Great Lie that failed (just) to destroy it. Two years on, after a complex process of selection and translation involving the efforts of many, I pass on this gift to the readers of *Scar on the Stone*.

This book is, therefore, not a war anthology in any conventional sense – that is, a volume confined to the time-frame of a war, focussing on the experience of soldier-poets and the wider poetic response to the civilian and military fronts. Rather, the work here spans roughly a half century, and with the exception of Mak Dizdar, all the poets are living. The sole criterion for the inclusion of the 22 poets has been artistic distinction; and organising a representative selection of each, based in most cases on the poet's own shortlist, I have been guided by considerations of artistic achievement rather than thematic appositeness. The earliest poems here date from the Nazi occupation and the first flush of Tito's new Yugoslavia; the latest, from after the war, belong to another country, Europe's newest independent nation, baptised in aggression and genocide. In between, Dizdar's poems, written in the sixties, hark back to the faithful of medieval Bosnia and, further still, to the land that was once a province of Roman Illyria. The schismatic Bosnian Church of the 13th to 15th centuries (sometimes known, incorrectly, as the Bogomils) straddled the Latin and Eastern rites, and was ruthlessly persecuted by Western ecclesiastical authority; most historians agree that its remnant lasted into Ottoman times, when Bosnians converted *en masse* to Islam. As for Illyria, this is the very land that Shakespeare transmutes into the bright Mediterranean nowhere of *Twelfth Night*.

As it turns out, about half the poems date from the onset of the break-up of Yugoslavia in June 1991. The ordering of the poets is such that there is general movement from prewar to wartime work; even so, the order was determined more by sensibility than chronology. A large proportion of the work up until Ferida Duraković's is prewar (though perhaps the most celebrated war poem in Bosnia itself – 'Why Venice Is Sinking' by Abdulah Sidran (pp.66-67) – comes near the beginning); thereafter, the poetry is mainly wartime, with the section of emergent poets, *New Voices* (pp.181-200), being entirely so. Occasionally, I have affixed a date to sharpen a poem's irony, but on balance thought it more fertile to let the reader surmise (where it is not obvious) on which side of the 1991 threshold a poem falls. A caveat: a good number of poems will resist such a determination. Much of Marko Vešovic's selection, for instance, might be construed as a response to the war; in fact, he wrote only prose during the siege, and the poems here are all prewar. Yet those in question gain from the aura of anticipation; and as with several of Semezdin Mehmedinović's, you wonder at poetry's uncanny ability, at certain historical moments, to foreshadow and even prophesy.

What was once known officially as Serbo-Croat is now a language without a common name in common use. It is called Bosnian, Croatian or Serbian depending on who or where you are. These names were always used in preference to the official term, even though most of the words in all three would have been roughly the same. 'Bosnian', however, tended before independence to denote the dialect, the peasant patois; and Bosnians of all backgrounds used the same Turkish words. In purely linguistic terms, the dialect continua of Serbo-Croat were no more complex than for any long-established mother tongue covering an area of similar size (Anglo-Scots, say). But, of course, the difference between an accent, a dialect and a language is vastly more complex than vocabulary, for questions of identity, cultural authority and statehood intrude. Language is a totem of personal and collective self-definition. Nowadays, in any event, Bosnian is the 'Serbo-Croat' spoken by all those who keep faith, in some sense, with Bosnia in its historic form. All the poets here, therefore, write in Bosnian.

The notion of keeping faith with Bosnia – in the sense of bearing witness to its suffering and significance – was also something that underlay my thinking on whom to invite as translators. All the translators here have a major interest in, and/or biographical connection to, Bosnia; or have lived the Adriatic region; or responded earlier to Bosnia's plight by contributing a poem to the Bloodaxe anthology *Klaonica: poems for Bosnia* (1993, edited by Ken Smith and Judi Benson). In the very choice of translators, then, I wanted to make a

small cumulative nod to the principle of what Mehmedinović calls
in one of his prose poems 'an engagement marked by *intellectual
morality*' (p.169). The widespread Western taboo that dichotomises
the writer as artist and citizen from the conduct of high politics, so
evident in the general literary quiescence in the face of the Bosnian
genocide, is just that – a social taboo, a matter of literary autism or
careerist caution, and not of course some dictum of artistic scruple,
as the epigraph poem by Nuala Ní Dhomhnaill (also the translator
of Duraković) dramatically illustrates. Part of my purpose, in other
words, was to bring together a number of poets and scholars for
whom the writ of this taboo did not run.

    Poetry, as the old chestnut has it, *is what gets lost in translation.*
Since apples are not oranges, who can doubt that there is some truth
in this? I do doubt, though, that many poets would put their hand to
the task if this was the *whole* truth. Yes, everything that is language-
specific in a poem is lost in translation. But every language has a
huge universal dimension – a zone of meanings shared with other
languages, to a greater or lesser extent, depending on their relative
positions on the great oak of language genealogy. However untrans-
latable their shades and nuances, *ljubav* in Bosnian, *grá* in Irish and
love do overlap. It is this universalist dimension that is the wire in
the high-wire act of translation. It is easy, of course, to fall on either
side of the wire – the over-literal, or the lax. But we should not for-
get that the best translations, like the prose and poetry of the King
James Bible, can be glorious indeed. In truth, much of the active
inner structure of image and sentence and idea – and underneath,
the universal idiom of thought and feeling – *can* be replicated; and
out of all this, too, something like an X-ray of the original all-per-
vading vision. 'Translators,' wrote Pushkin optimistically, 'are the
post-horses of enlightenment.'

    It is a truism that there are as many theories of translation as there
are translators. But I think it safe to say that all the translations here
belong to one general school. Each of the translators has attempted to
walk the wire between poetic integrity and faithfulness – between
doing it right within the music of English and doing right by the lit-
eral thrust of the original. The fashion for using a translation as a
springboard for the translator's own poetic riffs was eschewed. Given
the subject-matter of some of the poems, it could hardly have been
otherwise. Good translation demands not only a degree of ego-sub-
limation and imaginative affinity with the Other; but very often, and
no more so than with a poetry of witness, a sense of being placed
under exacting obligations where – as Ted Hughes once said of his

translations of the Hungarian János Pilinszky –'there is no question of introducing anything from the translator's own poetical medicine bag'. Clearly, the way poetic intensity was balanced with fidelity varied with the burden to be carried along the wire. Several translators had to grapple with work steeped in the untranslatable marinade of verse-music or vocal tone. But the idea that closeness to the spirit of the original tends to preclude translation of poetic merit is quite misplaced. Take, for instance, Francis Jones' scintillating translations of Dizdar. In a number he renders the medieval Bosnian into Middle English: the result of such scrupulousness is not a diminution but a dramatic increase in poetic authority.

Six of the translators worked directly from the Bosnian. The American poet Charles Simic, a native speaker, grew up in Serbia before emigrating to the United States; Francis Jones (University of Newcastle upon Tyne) and Ammiel Alcalay (City University of New York) are distinguished scholars and translators of Bosnian literature; the English poet John Hartley Williams lived for several years in the former Yugoslavia; and Antonela Glavinić and Ivana Djordjević are professional translators. The other eight translators, all poets, worked from the superb cribs – never less than lucid and nuanced – provided by Antonela Glavinić (nine poets) and Igor Klikovac (one poet). Such cribs involve a taxing tightrope of their own, on which the success of the final translations greatly depends. If they are to maximise the poetic quality of the final versions, they need to stick closely to the meaning and spirit of the original in precise and idiomatic English, which is nonetheless immediate, rough-hewn, even odd; and thereby to preserve both the native flavour of the language and the atmomsphere of the poet's style. In this way a raw sense of the strange original can be projected into the host language. Happily, all this was handled with impressive finesse.

The backdrop to this anthology – war, genocide, an unjust peace – made me balk at the usual format of the genre. One of the greatest losses in translation is so obvious as to approach invisibility: historical and cultural context. It is a loss almost wholly immune to the translator's skill. The essence of a language, ironically, is not entirely embodied in its words. This is particularly evident when the translation takes place between a small "peripheral" language and culture and the great transnational zone of English. The whole associative context of the smaller language falls by the wayside.

In the aftermath of such terrible events, therefore, was it enough to offer the poems alone, and go with the piety that poetry can always do its work single-handedly? What of the reader who knows little

of Bosnia, the former Yugoslavia or the wider Balkans? If such a
historico-cultural context could be added that made the poetry rich-
er for many readers, why not? What is the goal of poetry, even in
translation, if not a fullness of meaning? I saw no reason why the
native shadowlands of context might not be recouped somewhat by
stretching the format of the poetry anthology in a novel direction.

That is why, early on, I decided to include prose. With one ex-
ception, the pieces are all non-fiction. I have positioned them so as
to create narrative frame in dialectic with the poetry, one which
will illumine both individual poems and the anthology as a whole.
Not so much an argued, however, as an impressionistic narrative.
The prose suggests something of Bosnia under Tito; of the nature
of the nationalism that tore the country apart; of the death-camps
and the siege of Sarajevo; of the postwar aftermath. Having opted
for this procedure, I found that it enriched the volume in other ways.
It sets up a counterpoint of differing viewpoints: Bosnian and out-
sider, actuality and imagination, history and poetry. Those last two
contrasts engender a further line of counterpoint. What constitutes
the uniqueness of poetry, what is its special place on the psychic
continuum of human being? What is its anthropological forte, as
Joseph Brodsky once asked, in comparison to other discourses?

Scar on the Stone makes it more than usually plain that poetry is
not omnipotent. No poem could replicate the capaciousness of his-
torical witness allied to a perfect pitching of reticence and psalmic
passion across the whole of *The Tenth Circle of Hell* (pp.108-16). A
poem could deal with the same experience, if Omarska had befallen
the poet; what it did say might be even more illuminating; but it
could not, quite obviously, obtain to the same prosaic virtues. To
apprehend the power of any medium you must acknowledge its
boundaries. What, then, is the frontier between poetry and other
forms of writing? The juxtapositions of this anthology proffer, I
think, some hints and insights. In doing so, the book also suggests
how rich the cross-fertilisation of genres can be.

So my overall aim has been to assemble a book which can appeal
equally to the reader interested in poetry and the reader simply
interested in Bosnia. Why should the country's poetry not feel as
accessible as the memoirs, the studies, the apologias about Bosnia
that are already accumulating? Why should poetry, of all things, be
assumed to have abandoned the general reader? Even as poets in
their Western citadel assert the centrality of poetry – literary, lin-
guistic, psychic, cultural, spiritual, etc – they are resigned to its *de
facto* ghetto within the modern mainstream, to the drift of its isola-

tion from the wider community. It is a curious pass for 'the most beautiful and serious use of human breath' (Peter Levi). There are deep-seated civilisational reasons, but even before these kick in half the battle is lost to preconception.

The steadfast speech articulation known as poetry – the prime means of showing forth the suppleness of a single consciousness faced with the music of what happens – has, in part, become Poetry, an off-putting cultural phenomenon, burdened with the albatross of worthiness and excess difficulty. Unjust in the case of the best, of course, but it is a chicken-and-egg situation: isolated from the main-stream, the taste and ear for the art must diminish therein. Nonetheless, an anthology such as this, intersecting with a general awareness of Bosnia, can seek to serve as a bridge, albeit small, between the poetic ghetto and the wider culture. That is the final reason I wanted the narrative momentum occasioned by the interplay of the poetry and prose: it is more inviting to the general reader because, quite simply, it makes for a better read.

I open the anthology with two extracts from Czesław Miłosz's *The Witness of Poetry* because they suggest the historical conditions under which poetry was written in the Bosnia of 1992-95 (see p.5). Miłosz is writing about Polish poetry under the Nazi occupation, as a case study of 'the encounter of the European poet with the hell of the twentieth century', but his discussion has relevance for the whole of Occupied Europe. The poetry of Occupied Europe is, then, the par-allel to which we should turn regarding the wartime poetry in the following pages. The Bosnian poet of the besieged cites and ravaged countryside encountered the same hell – a hell that Europe West of the Iron Curtain had nearly forgotten.

The work after 1991 may therefore be seen as cognate with the broader literature of the Occupation, Resistance and Holocaust. *Scar on the Stone* is, in fact, the first anthology of poetry from the Bosnian war to have appeared in any language. (It is also, very probably, the first ever anthology of Bosnian poetry in English to have been published outside the former Yugoslavia). Unquestionably, the war poetry issues from that background atmospheric described by Miłosz, what might be described as war's revelatory and fundamental order: the twin annunciations, experienced on the poet's own skin, of the the hierarchical nature of reality and the consequent fragility of all civilisation. How this is registered, therefore, seems of major his-torical and literary interest. What news from the latest encounter with twentieth-century barbarity?

The poetry will speak for itself, of course – in its own idiom of meaning, the shot-silk of the particular and general. But several themes seem to me striking enough to warrant some brief comment. These are not so much fully immanent in single poems as evident in the way a number of moments in the poetry interface with the historical conditions described by Miłosz. As with the classic literature of Second World War extremity, such messages emerge as if out of a bottle launched on the remote shores of the inhuman. They not only issue from humanity in ruins: they issue a challenge to our peaceable lexicon about the role of literature as an beneficent force in history.

One such motif concerns the "postmodern" commodification of tragedy. Several poems and prose poems (I am thinking of a number by Mehmedinović and Duraković) come not to praise the postmodern, but to bury it. Postmodernism, of course, is one of the great weasel words of our *fin de siècle* – part of its glamour stems from imprecision – but it essentially involves a denial of Miłosz's observation that 'all reality is hierarchical', and privileges a new order of appearance – surface, image, incoherence, spectacle, *depthlessness* – over the immemorial sense of truth as a search for an architecture of significant *depth*, involving gradations of interiority, essence, coherence and authenticity. The classic locus of postmodernism is mass culture; its prime medium is the mass media; its characteristic devices are collage, intertextuality and pastiche. Cutting to the heart of the matter, it can be summarised thus: the cultural policy of commodification, the supra-capitalist process now quickening across the globe, reducing all to its use, even the human genome. Everything is "flattened" because everything is the same: a commodity. Even the "tragedies" on our television screens.

In Sarajevo, however, we glimpse how this process looks from outside the charmed circle of postmodern "securities". For once, it is the modern European poet who witnesses the commodification of tragedy, the massacre in the street turned into surface fodder for the media: 'The camera empties an image of psychological content and turns it into information' (p.176). Even the theses of visiting Western intellectuals 'turn war into a war game' by glozing the Munch-screams of the populace. Yet the Sarajevo of these pages also reveals the Achilles heel of all commodification. *Death* cannot be flattened. It is the bull's eye that enforces the spiral gradations of depth; the cipher that insists on 'a hierarchy of needs'. 'You call this place "hell"/ and run away; telling yourself/ that outwith Sarajevo, death is unknown' (p.173). Indeed, it is one of the serendipities of the book that the Great Zero sings out from beginning to end, through war and peace. But it is the background reality of the war work that must pose a challenge to the theorists of surface. The poem of 'universal endangerment' does not enhance reality, reality enhances it. War and genocide, enforcing 'a great simplification', begin to look like a unexpected cul-de-sac for the privileging of postmodern discourse.

There are two other motifs here strongly reminiscent of the literature of twentieth-century catastrophe. One is the apprehension of silence, speech in dialectic with the unutterable. In Ranko Sladojević's selection, for instance, a sense of the inner muteness and deafness enforced by the siege – war as an autism overwhelming the spirit – is powerfully conveyed. To paraphrase George Steiner, the word borders on night. For me this is the true sense of Adorno's famous dictum, 'No poetry after Auschwitz': not that poetry cannot or should not be written (a palpable absurdity), but that we must recognise that there are zones of reality which can never obtain to poetic, or indeed any verbal, expression. Reality eludes language, yet in approaching the borderlands of silence Sladojević gives expression, ironically, to the common experience of the besieged.

This distrust of the efficacy of language, the cloth from which all knowledge is cut, is but a sub-category of a second and more comprehensive alienation. Namely, a mistrust of the civilising power of culture itself, the very matrix of humane aspiration; an accusation glimpsed right across the anthology. In 'Anti-Mauberley', Hamdija Demirović, now working for the War Crimes Tribunal in The Hague, revisits Ezra Pound's First World War classic, 'Hugh Selwyn Mauberley', and reinvigorates the image of culture's deceit to fierce and epitomising effect. And if culture is sometimes put on trial as a sham, it is also revealed, no less than flesh, as poignant dust. 'Ruins whose dust is the sole certainty of what is to come': thus Aneta Benac-Krstić on the destruction of her grandparents' house in 'A Broken Honeycomb' (p.187). We see books used for fuel and barricades, and the treasures of the National Library ending in the ash-pit. As for the immaterial life of ideas, 'to every question fire provides/ a quick simplified answer' (p.185). There is, truly, no continuing city.

Yet the poetry of the Bosnian war assembled here diverges in one major respect from the Occupation picture adumbrated by Miłosz. For the most part, he notes, Polish poetry during the War – the main underground genre, owing to its compactness – belongs stylistically to the pre-war period, like the literature of the prisons and concentration camps generally. Today we would grant almost all of it documentary and ethical value, rather than artistic distinction. In seeking to convey a new order of terror, the old repertoire of notions and techniques failed to grasp the shock of the unprecedented, and the resulting inadequacies are all the more apparent in the face of the subject-matter. It was more of a gasping for air, a ventilation of agony and morale, than a fashioning of durable breath. It is only after the War that certain Polish poets, possessed of a necessary detachment, find the new stylistic means adequate to the experience.

Here, however, a quite different pattern of technique and achieved contemporaneousness is evident, one suggesting both the sophistication of individual talents and the evolution of poetic *donneés* after a half-century in the shadow of World War and Cold War. You will search in vain for the merely documentary, hortatory or engagé. (Granted, much of the wider poetic and literary picture probably does conform to the Polish model.) As Mehmedinović observes in a prose poem, 'because the gaze has been so violently disrupted in this city', the merely descriptive is of no artistic value. Instead, you sense a number of the country's best poets marooned in the midst of a war, digging deep into imaginative resource and coming up with work not merely true to the evil of the hour, but strong enough to outlast it. Moreover, because the inner gaze engendered by the war was anything but documentary, the war poems here register the surreality of common experience more authentically. 'Everyone in Sarajevo, accustomed to death,' continues Mehmedinović, 'lives through so many transcendental experiences that they have already become initiates of some deviant form of Buddhism. If the aggression lasts another month or so, many of them will believe that a chestnut falling on Wilson's Promenade carries more weight than a grenade.' In fact, it lasted two more years. Reading these pages, one appreciates the sheer challenge of depicting elemental cruelty, whether in Warsaw or Belsen, Sarajevo or Omarska.

Enter Radovan Karadžić. Poet and war criminal, he is the smirking sunflower of the Bosnian killing fields. To my mind, the several allusions here possess the irresistible symbolism of a children's writer turned ring-leader for a supreme criminality. Though no one took much notice of him, Karadzic the pre-war poet was something more than a mere aspirant: he published three collections of poems (*Mad Spear*, 1968; *Bloated Century*, 1971; *Black Fairy Tale*, 1989), as well as two volumes of poetry for children; and I have an anthology of Serbian poetry of the former Yugoslavia, published in Sarajevo in 1991 and edited by a respected poet, which includes a middling lyric of his entitled 'Doppelgänger'. A creature of connections, he was one of a claque of mediocre "rural" writers oxygenated by the patronage of the publishing system. A line from one of his early poems, like some macabre boomeranging of poetic licence, actually became a well-known slogan for the genocide: 'Take no pity let's go/ kill that scum down in the city.' How does a children's writer come to orchestrate the death of tens of thousands of children, including two thousand during the siege of Sarajevo which he personally directed?

Karadžić thus exemplifies one of most striking aspects of a war which included updates of trench warfare, Guernica and My Lai: the integral role of writers in resurrecting, then mobilising, the undead corpse of Serb nationalism. Not only as dangerous opinion-mongers, but as actual leaders in positions of authority over the commission of crime. 'This is probably the only war in history planned and led by writers,' Vešović has commented. Though little remarked upon by Western writers, the phenomenon is obvious in Bosnia, and has strong roots in a Wagnerian mythopoetics fusing oral epic, folklore, archaic Christianity and nationalism. In this sense, the example of Karadžić simply confirms that poetry and virtue are not the same, and iterates the truth of what Italian novelist Ignazio Silone wrote in the immediate aftermath of the Second World War: 'Writers, artists and intellectuals in general have no right whatever to boast of any disinterested, foresighted or courageous part played by them in the sad decades through which we have passed ... It is certainly dangerous and difficult to talk of a moral life in any country; but in any case it would be extremely hazardous to suggest that it coincided with that of a country's intellectual life.'

In another sense, however, the example of Karadžić has a still darker message. He unsettles the very notion of the *general* beneficence of literature. If good poetry is the pearl, what of the oyster, the undistinguished bulk? Is it not the case, and not merely in places like the Soviet Union and Bosnia, that literature, like the personalities who create it, can both cherish and endanger values? Is our view of the arts too rosy?

We in the 'settled' world have got used to speaking of the arts as if they were a kind of moral immune system for the body politic. Is this true? Only, I think, if the richness of the metaphor is borne in mind. An immune system works best when the body is healthy; when it sickens, the system becomes both more important and less efficacious. Then, in certain scenarios like AIDS, the immune system itself can be the cause of illness. This is what happened in the former Yugoslavia: it contracted a full-blown case of literary AIDS.

Thrown into a war situation, the actual moral character of those living through it shows up as if on an X-ray: their courage or cowardice, rectitude or lack of scruple, charity or egoism: and of course this is just as true of writers and what they write, and (sometimes) have written before. For if self-transcendence is the essence of imagination, it is also the basis of licence. Freed of an ethical mooring, literature can sail swiftly into the licentious under the trade winds of the moment. Simone Weil argued that just such a weakening of values in literature had occurred in the run-up to the Second World War, and was a prime factor in its outbreak. 'Licence has always entranced men and that is why, throughout history, cities have been sacked. But the sacking of cities has not always had its equivalent in literature.' In his transition from minor poet to major war criminal, Karadžić symbolises the same symbiosis operating in the destruction of Yugoslavia.

When I began this anthology, I wondered if I might come across a poet in whose *work* artistic distinction and ethical licence coexisted. It never turned up, and I still think that the conjunction of the two can never be found in poetry worthy of the name because it is alien to the intimate grain of the art. The reason is exactly as Joseph Brodsky formulated it in his 1988 Nobel Lecture: 'It is not so much that virtue does not constitute a guarantee for producing a masterpiece, as that evil, especially political evil, is always a bad stylist.' And why is it a bad stylist? Because social wickedness, on a personal level, is always bound up with the suppression of one's individuality in the name of some framing conformity, such as identity, economy or ideology. Indeed, as Danilo Kiš saw all too well (pp.77-79), the process of identity overwhelming individuality is a formula both for collective delusion and literary kitsch.

   This loss of individual consciousness in the form of a slavish worship of national origins engulfed Yugoslavia as a mass phenomenon from the mid-eighties onwards. It is the psychic soil from which the genocide of the Muslims grew, since its mirror-image is the dehumanisation of others. It is also pure poison to the spirit of individuality on which all art thrives. Identity does not equal individuality, and "belonging" is rarely the best means for an artist to speak to the complexities of others.

   As the art critic Robert Hughes has remarked, 'One makes art to allow the unknown self – unknown to others, but also to the artist – to speak; the work gropes to such a resolution...Identity says nothing about deep aesthetic ordering; such ordering is conscious and

existential, and identity is an accident.' It is precisely in this sense
that identity is an anathema to poetry – and more so, arguably, than in
other arts, due to its closeness to the single human voice. Identity
always involves some collectivisation of sensibility; whereas poetic
speech seeks to clone the uniqueness of a single consciousness. In
a world swept by mass cultural phenomena, part of poetry's stead-
fastness lies in its preservation of this precious sense of human scale.
Its native grain is the single voice speaking to the single ear; and
like the lichen threatened by acid rain, the achieved poem cannot
abide the siren-song of collective enchantment.

Bosnia was the Spanish Civil War of our time. It represented, and
still represents, a clash between the open and the closed society, a
modern polity aspiring to pluralism and democracy, and one predi-
cated on hatred and 'purity' – between the ideals of the Enlightenment
and the dark cult of chauvinism. But unlike Spain, or even Vietnam,
Bosnia never quite became a *cause célèbre* for artists and intellec-
tuals abroad, apart from a small minority, having failed somehow
to muster a critical mass of ethical imagination. Notwithstanding
the important rôle of Susan Sontag and some dedicated journalists,
why were there so few outside writers on the ground, why so little
sense of a galvanised and firsthand solidarity? Where were the
Hemingways and Dos Passos, the Pazs and Koestlers and Spenders,
the Orwells and Audens, the Malraux and Weils?

In the following pages we encounter not the Chorus of identity
but the suppleness of the single sensibility. That is why I have not
included confessional labels in the biographical notes. The relation
of the poets here to issues of upbringing and belief is as complex as
anywhere else. Nonetheless, for the record (but not in order), the
overall confessional profile of the first fourteen poets is as follows:
eight of Muslim background, four of Orthodox, two of Catholic.
As for the New Voices section, I never bothered checking up on
backgrounds, and a guess based on names is unreliable. A number
fought in the war to defeat the final logic of such categorisations.
'Citizens of Bosnia' will have to do.

MAK DIZDAR

Translations by FRANCIS R. JONES

Mak Dizdar (1917-71) is Bosnia's most outstanding 20th-century poet. Born in Stolac, Herzegovina, he attended Sarajevo University and fought in Tito's Resistance during the Second World War. A post office clerk before the war, he subsequently worked as a journalist and literary editor. *Stone Sleeper*, published in various revisions from 1966, is his key work. It is a complex masterpiece rooted in the mystery of the schismatic Bosnian Church of the Middle Ages and its resistance to the heretic-killers of the established church – a mystery crucial to our understanding of modern Bosnia's strengths and tribulations.

Stone Sleeper – from which these selections are taken – is not only a work of poetry. It is also an act of scholarship, a journey into a period and a people about which no two historians agree. More precisely, it is a journey only a poet-scholar could have undertaken, for only the scholar knows the way to this land – the Bosnian faithful, their enigmatic tombs, their still more enigmatic faith – and only the poet can recreate what lies there.

Main publications: *Vidopoljska Night* (1936), *The Return* (1958), *The Cruelty of a Circle* (1960), *Knees for Madonna* (1963), *Miniatures* (1965), *Islands* (1966), and *Stone Sleeper* (1966).

Text about a land

> *Pars fuit Illyriae, quam nunc vocat incola Bosnam,*
> *Dura, sed argenti munere dives humus.*
> *Non illic virides spacioso margine campi,*
> *Nec sata qui multo foenere reddat ager.*
> *Sed rigidi montes, sed saxa minantia coleo,*
> *Castella et summis imposita alta iugis.*

> There was a part of Illyria, now called Bosnia by its inhabitants,
>   Hard, but its ground rich with the gift of silver.
> No wide-edged green plains there,
>   Nor fields which yield crops of much value.
> But rugged mountains, beetling rock-pinnacles,
>   And tall castles perched on tops of ridges.

IANI PANNONI QUINQUE: *Elegarium Liber* (El. VI)

Once upon a time a worthy questioner asked:
Forgive me who is and what sir
Where is
Whence and
Whither sir
Prithee sir
Is this
Bosnia

The questioned swiftly replied in this wise:
Forgive me there once was a land sir called Bosnia

A fasting a frosty a
Footsore a drossy a
Land forgive me
That wakes from sleep sir
With a
Defiant
Sneer

A word on man

First

Born in a body barred in with veins
Dreaming that seven heavens descend

Barred in a heart bound into brains
Dreaming the sun in dark without end

Bound in your skin ground into bones
Where is the bridge

To heaven's thrones?

Second

Barred in a ribcage of silver your chains
Be ye so mighty no whiter than serf

Born in a body barred in with veins
Dreaming a union of heaven and earth

Cast out of heaven you thirst wine and bread
When will your home

Be your homeland instead?

Note: Medieval Balkan dualism saw mortals as fallen angels, expelled from heaven and imprisoned in human bodies. Nor did they return to heaven when they died, their souls stayed with their bodies until the Last Judgement.

Third

Barred in with bones woven in flesh
Soon will your bones poke through this mesh

Cast out of heaven you crave wine and bread
Stone and smoke's all you get instead

I see your one hand but where is the other
Was it lifted

To kill its brother?

Fourth

Barred in a heart bound in a brain
Black your cave the sun you crave

Dreaming of heaven near once again
Your drunken body weaves through the leaves

Bound in blood consumed by roots
In this kolo of sorrow

Do you lead
Or follow?

Fifth

In this *kolo* of sorrow not leader not led
You're a tavern of carrion a maggots' bed

Robbed from its body the tomb acts alone
But when will this body

Be an act of its own?

Recognition

For in the deepest depths of death
        the colours will be clearer then

Text about the hunt

An underground water wakes from deepest sleep breaks free
        and streams through a clear and glorious dawn
        towards a distant river
        towards a weary
        sea

Meekly tripping between the forest's golden green the fawn
        will not stop until her course
        bring her to her spring
        her source

Slipping between the ochre saplings the flustered roe
        seeks a vanished whisper seeks the fleeting days
        that pass between the dimlit grass
        that flit between the frets
        of grassy nets

I see that stag beguiled by the eyes of the doe
        entranced by her glance till sunset come
        his limbs grow numb
        his tread
        go red

A tall horseman masters seething spaces of unrest
        Handsome Dumb with deep desire Blind
        without a sound he tramps behind
        the baying and howling of hounds
        panting thirsty straining for the blood of future
        battlegrounds

I see it all in a second In this day's sun
    As if with a glance
    Of a hand
    And

I know that starveling sparkling spring will never enter its distant delta
    its gentle shelter I know that source
    will never caress its pebble of pure
    quartz

The restive doe will never hear the tiny cry that greets
    her trails her tails her through the cover
    will never hear the bleats
    of mother

No more will the stag climb the cliff and never again
    will he bell his reply to the green cry
    of the green
    rain

Nor will the tall horseman huntsman splendid in his battledress
    amid the cavalcade and all its show
    ever loose that battle arrow
    from his bended
    bow

For in that single instant that split second
    when rapt in self all were hunters
    and utterly
    alone

I Grubač the hewer did hunt these hunters down threads unseen
    them I writ with humble wit them I truly drew
    in the height
    in the white
    of this stone

Note: Master Grubač, who worked in the mid-15th century, is one of the most cel-
ebrated *stećci* (tombstone) sculptors whose name is known to us. He is buried in
the necropolis of Boljuni near Stolac, where in life he carved a *stećak* with an
elaborate hunting scene.

Sun

A young sun on the run from his father
  made house on a heath between two icy peaks

Not knowing who he was we glanced askance at first

He rolled up his sleeves and ploughed the earth good and deep
  right down to her bowels right down to her heart

Resting after his efforts he waved a friendly hand
  then up he soared above the dark just like a hawk

And he shone on every byway on every track and fork
  showing us his furrows and our faces in his blaze

Then we embraced as if at a long-awaited sign

We came together and became as one
  we ate and drank as if we'd always done

He wasn't just a summer caller this sun of ours
  even the barren valley blossomed with flowers

All of a sudden our young sun stole away from us

Where he went to why and how
  only the good Lord knows that now

We might have forgotten him like some lucky chance
  (easy come and easy go)
  if we weren't still warming the whole of our soul

By the heat of his long-gone golden hands

Note: The Bosnian Church appears to have taught that the earth had entered its final age, as foretold in the Book of Revelation, when the world was given over to darkness, i.e. to Satan. Soon, however, Christ – the light – would defeat Satan forever. There are strong echoes of sun-worship here. One source may be the cult of the sun-god Mithras, which was especially popular with Roman legionaries; many legionaries, once they had finished service, were rewarded with grants of land in what later came to be known as Bosnia.

Moon

From the thick dark of a weary day the tender
    young face of a moon appeared above our heads

Now he sails the whole wide reach of his sky
    waking those who have lost themselves

Before he tires of his shining journey
    before his waxing falls out of step

    (before he's swathed on every side
    in white and silver hair)

Carve his sign in the soft white of limestone
    so you may absorb as faithfully as can be

The image of your infinite pain and hope

Text about time

Long have I lain here before thee
And after thee
Long shall I lie

Long
Have the grasses my bones
Long
Have the worms my flesh
Long
Have I gained a thousand names
Long
Have I forgot my name

Long have I lain here before thee
And after thee
Long shall I lie

Note: The first verse comes from the tombstone of a certain Stipko Radosalić
in a cemetery near the village of Ljubinje. The *stećak* also shows a crescent
moon: the boat that will eventually carry the dead person to the after-life.

Rain

We need to learn again
        to listen to the rain the rain

We need to disenstone ourselves
        and eyes straight to walk unwavering through the city gate

We need to uncover the lost paths
        that pass through the blond grass

We need to caress the poppies and ants
        panicking in this plenty of plants

We need to wash ourselves anew
        and dream in clean drops of dawn dew

We need to swoon
        between the dark tresses of grassy hair

We need to stand a while beside our sun
        and grow as tall as our shadow

We need to meet our own hearts again
        that fled so long ago

We need to disenstone ourselves
        and eyes straight to walk unwavering through this stone
                          city's stone gate

We need to wish with all our might
        and listen all night to the rain the rain the righteous rain

The city gate: The faithful of the Bosnian Church saw themselves as the righteous described in the Book of Revelation: on Judgement Day they would be taken from their graves, and they alone would be led into the New Jerusalem. See Revelation XXI.

The Rightwise

Walking thorough the erthe
Thorough the night and light
He beheld wickednesse
He beheld sicknesse

And he did hele hurtes

And then he raysed up his hedde
To heaven he spake a worde
He begged that the secret be seid
About this gravewards roade

He begged that the secret be seid

But only the stillnesse of ledde
Did fille the welkins bowle
Alas the worde was heard
Only by those with no soule

Only by those with no soule

Discorde delighted the dragoun
The fiery flying serpent
The worde it fell as dedd
On the deffnesse of the dark

The worde it fell as dedd

He descended into himselfe
Depe in the catacombes
Where houndes do rende the flesh
After the hecatombes

Where houndes do rende the flesh

And his body did embarke
On its voyauge thorough the dark
But a voyce did falle below
And ring forth thorough the stillnesse

Did ring forth thorough the stillnesse

A voyce which forever flyeth
Which up to heaven hyeth

Yea which forever flyeth

Text on a watershed

1

In this good worldes joyes
I Good Abel Joyce was ay good able to rejoyce

and in that short summer still he sought him flowers
and when he fought was fraught with smart still he stale him stars

all through the strife of life his way he did not rue
behind the scorching sun he saw the heavens blue

when time him claimed he stopped betime dropped by the way
but all he found in his fall was the gloom of the tomb

now he needeth ne man ne thing
in his blue glade in his cool shade

now he needeth ne bread ne wine
there they be not sated there they do not pine

there falleth no rain there shineth no sun

no need hath he no more save one
to reach the havens of the sun

2

Pardon me
that I pray that ye

and my brethren my fellows my betters
do come to my door do visit me

that I pray that godmother motherlaw aunt and bride
do speak my name keep me in mind pass at times by my side

for once I was the same as ye
and as I am so shall ye be

Note: In the original, Abel Joyce is Radojica Bjelić: I chose to keep the original word-play rather than his original name. The first two lines of Part 1 and the last two lines of Part 2 are written on his tomb, in Staro Selo near Donji Vakuf.

Kolo of sorrow

How long the kolo from hollow to hollow
How long the sorrow from kolo to kolo

How long the dread from stead to stead
How long the tombs from coomb to coomb

How long the blood we are judged to pay
How long the deaths till the judgement day

How long the kolo from hollow to hollow
How long the sorrow from kolo to kolo

Kolo to kolo from sorrow to sorrow

The *kolo* is the South Slav round dance. Carvings on the tombs show that it has remained unchanged since medieval times.

Radimlja

the vine and its branches

Present here is He
Who said for verily it is writ
I am the true vine and my Father is the husbandman and Every
                                                    branch in me
That beareth not fruit I shall take away
But that the field wax fat the fruit be sweeter the root be deeper
The branch that beareth
I shall purge

Now ye are clean through the word which I have spoken unto you
Therefore cast ye your brute
Matter into this fiery flame Abide thus in me
And I most surely in you
As in those I abode in of old as in those whom I loved true
For I am the vine and ye
Are the fruit

Present here is He
Who is ever ready for word and deed
Whose Word once heard doth heal
Whose Deed doth bite like white
Hot steel

Since ages past Thou awaitest me
Thou waitest and Thee I surely see
For I am thine
I fall towards Thee
Through the white
Of Thy vine

Radimlja, near Stolac, is probably the finest medieval necropolis in Bosnia.
Vines laden with grapes are a frequent motif on *stećci*. See John XV. 1-4.

the gate

Here just guests we stand out still
Although we should have crossed into a ring of light
And passed at last through a strait gate in order to return
Out of this naked body into the body eterne

When I happened by this evening late
Unbidden He said unto me

I am that gate and at it enter into Me as I now into thee
So he spoke but where is the mouth of the lock where the finger of
                    the one true key for the gate to the burning stair?
I grope in the grass I scour my skull for the one blue key
Seeking a path through spring's flowers past death's scythes searching
                                        for that golden door
I stoop through ants and plants through sooth and untruth I seek
                                                and find
But when I raise my hand to the lock who betrays my desperate quest?

This dark side of the door an ill wind prowls a foul wind howls
I forsake my sister and brother forsake my father and mother
between the beasts and the men
To seek my essence my pillar of blinding incandescence
How in this world must I find that word
What would be in the finding?

Unbidden he said unto me
Enter ye into Me for I am that shining gate But still
I wait I lie I rot I die upon this sill
And the wind the wind the wind

If the gate of the word is just a dream a fairy tale
Still I will not leave this door
Here I want to live once more
This supreme
Dream

[See Matthew VII. 14]

the fourth horseman

It is time to think of time
As we gag at death's decay her stinking slime
It is time to think of time
As mighty waters rush towards us
See them crush and devour her puny power
Lo it is time to think in time
For a wind a swift wind a dragon-wind
Shall swoop upon us this evil day
For time is a fire so let it scour us let it devour us
Lo it is time to enter into this time
Because it hath but a short time
And time shall be no longer

[See Revelation VI. 7-8]

Cossara

When the hunters hunt her through the thorny brake
With my hands I build a bridge for her to take

Though they drive her onward through each muddy stream
She is drawing closer strange though it may seem

Now beneath the sword they put her head so pure
In yourself you're tall in me you're strong and sure

Still you are not dumb although you are no more
In the sky her star

Shines like a crimson scar

Gorchin

Here lyeth
Gorchin soldier
In his owen lande
In a straungers
Estate

I was on lyf
Yet deth I hailed
By day and nighte

Ne fly wolde I harme
Yet I went
For a soldier

I foght
In warres five on five
Withouten buckler or maile
Ay alle at ones
Gorchin
Was ne more

I sterved of straunge sicknesse

Ne pyke ne perced me
Ne arrowe ne slewe me
Ne sworde
Ne smote me

I sterved of sicknesse
Withouten hele

I loved
But my lasse was
Into bondage taken

If thou Cossara meetest
Upon the paths
Of our Lorde
Tell her
I bid thee
That I my troth
Did kepe

A text about the five

Four men leading one man bound
One man whom the four men hound

Four men's faces dour and dire
Over water over wire

On they scoff and on they trough
Through each thread and through their bread

Through each hedge and through each Y
Until freedom us untie

Past the homes and past the tombs
Through the earth and through the sky

Four men leading one man bound
One man whom the four men hound

One man counted bound and led
One man whom the four men dread

Note: This poem dates from 1940-41, at the height of this century's first rape of
Bosnia. To guard against the risk of it being read by the Ustaša or Nazi occupiers,
Dizdar wrote it in the Arabic-based *alhamiya* ('foreign') script, thus making it
seem like a religious text. *Alhamiya* was the main script used for the Bosnian
language under the Turkish occupation, from the early 15th to the late 19th
century. *Through each Y:* the medieval Bosnian Church tried to simplify the
Old Slavonic script in order to make it closer to spoken Bosnian. One reform
was to scrap the silent letter Y.

FRANCIS R. JONES

FROM Return (1994)

Collar turned up, hunched against the swirling snow, I passed the second pole and the snap of its wind-taut tricolour and red star. Inside the customs hall, the Slovenian frontier guard, his face expressionless under the ill-fitting grey cap with its red enamel star, reached for my passport.

'*Englez?*'

'*Da.*'

He flicked through, stopped at a page full of visas: 'Student?'

'*Da.*'

'*U Sarajevu?*'

I nodded.

'*Autostop?*'

I nodded again. His face still set, he stamped and returned the passport, then:

'*Dodji.*' (Come with me.)

At the far end of the hall, a dozen men in open-necked shirts, some middle-aged and grizzled in ill-fitting crimplene suits, others longer-haired and clean-shaven, in the Yugoslav youth uniform of blue jeans and black leather jacket, were standing smoking.

'This Englishman is going to Bosnia. Have you got room?'

One of the older men, obviously the group leader, nodded: '*Nema problema.*'

The border guard offered his outstretched hand with a grin: '*Hajde momče, sretan put.*' (Have a good journey, lad.)

As they finished their cigarettes, we exchanged journeys – where are you coming from, where are you going – with the quiet camaraderie of long-distance travellers by night, when the world is no more than a ribbon of asphalt in the headlamp beams.

The men were gastarbeiters, migrant workers returning by coach to their Bosnian villages from the factories of the Ruhr. For this one month a year they would be home: to see mother, father and sisters again, brothers too young for exile, maybe even wife and children. To work a little further on the tile-clad breezeblock mansion with its wrought iron balconies, which was slowly but surely dwarfing the wood and plaster farmstead where they, their parents and grandparents were born. Or to sit all day in the kafana, regaling those who did not have the get-up-and-go with rounds of plum brandy and sweet coffee, bragging of blonde girlfriends and Siemens sound systems. The deutschmarks they bore financed an extended network of dependants, supplementing the scant pensions of retired parents, enabling younger brothers and sisters to stay on at school or college. Less apparent but more important, perhaps, they kept the local economy alive, providing work for the building trade, or subsidising their relatives to run the little farms that patchworked the fertile Bosnian hills.

The leader ground his cigarette stub under his heel, and turned to go. Outside stood the coach, engine revving ready, wipers swishing away the snow. Our group was the last to board: the doors closed with a hiss behind us. As I swung off my rucksack and settled into a free seat, still grinning with elation – all night and three hundred winding miles on a warm coach – the driver hauled out and down into the snowy night, then snapped on the cassette player.

'*Hajde, pij!*'

I raised the proffered bottle to my lips, expecting the searing of pure spirit, but instead a gentle warmth and a taste plummier than the ripest of plums suffused through me.

'It's excellent – what is it?'

'*Meka šljivovica* – single-distilled. My uncle makes it, up above Tuzla. *Pij još* – drink some more!

The driver turned up the cassette, and the agonised lilt of the *sevdalinka* soared through the coach. Wavering to its climax along the brink of discord, the music reached beyond the words lamenting an impossible love: it sang the bitter sweetness of existence, the pain of life balanced on a knife-edge against the beauty of song as long as the song lasts. As the bus plunged and twisted downwards through the Alpine night, it was the *sevdalinka* which swept me back, which sang me the reason for my return.

In the early hours, the coach left the Croatian flatlands and began winding into Bosnia's wooded valleys. Between waking and sleep, I had the sensation of coming home: even in darkness, through glass, I could feel the comforting bulk of those fertile hills. The coach stopped every half-hour or so to drop one or two men at a time at a shuttered roadside kafana, at a ramshackle farm with wood shingle roofs and a single light burning in an upstairs room, or at an unmetalled, unsignposted track climbing into the darkness by the rustle of rushing water. Or in a village, where post-war cement-on-breezeblock farmsteads clustered round a few streets of wood-framed claybrick houses with thick-walled courtyards, some of them with overhanging upper storeys and ancient slatted windows (designed, in the days of purdah, so that women could see into the street without being seen); where the streets met, there was a white-washed mosque and a drab glass-and-steel kiosk for bread or newspapers.

Soon after lightfall I too stepped out, a mere hundred miles from Sarajevo. I had heard of Jajce, of course. In this little enclave the medieval kings of Bosnia had been crowned; here, in 1943, Tito's Partisans, yet to take a major town from the Germans, had formed the optimistic government of free Yugoslavia; and it boasted a spectacular waterfall. Grey through the thin, drifting snow, the waterfall may have impressed me; but all I remember, fifteen years on, is the restless fatigue of a night of travel and fragmented sleep. I returned to the roadside, and held out my sign.

Next morning, back in the hostel, my British roommate and I see off our hangovers with a pan of Turkish coffee, brewed thick, black and sweet on the little hotplate beneath the washbasin. Then we go down to the street. Bob is off to the library, but I stop at the newspaper kiosk by the traffic lights, and come back up in the jerking lift which I still ride in my dreams, especially of late. I spread the newspaper and the map, still a little damp, on the desk overlooking the flat roof (covered in the shoes and bottles which plummet past our window when the parties on upper floors really get going), and start to star the likely 'Rooms for Let'.

Time slips. In another March, another room, the same sun breaks between snow-squalls to light the same map's tiny brown-and-yellow mosques, churches, municipal buildings, its parks with their little green trees, its child's train chugging along a railway line. It blends with the shaft of watery light which streams, fifteen years before, from beyond the Ilidža road, beyond the grown-ups' railway and the distant ridge, to illuminate the street names I've just underlined: Pećina, Panina Kula, Golobrdica, Pirin Brijeg...

The plan which paved my return had a double justification. By renting a room, Hanneke could join me here (we would probably have to pretend we were married, but intuition told us – even then – that this was less of a lie than an act of faith in the future). And by moving into the old town, I hoped to get closer to Bosnia's people, her past, a way of life missing from the concrete towerblock by the tramline.

The cliché picture of Tito's Yugoslavia, then as now, was one of a nation of bridged divides (though no one could have suspected then how rickety the bridges were): between Europe and Asia Minor, Christianity and Islam, Habsburg Central Europe and the Ottoman Balkans. And yet, to me then, these contrasts, though piquant, were a picturesque backdrop – the stage, perhaps, but not the drama itself. The divides I felt most keenly were not these ancient faultlines of geography, but ones of the mind: between conformity and dissent, materialism and the intellect, modernity and tradition.

On one side of this divide, the unquestioning conformity of most of my fellow students, their lack of dissent from the twin goods of materialism and Party, could be stifling. Their ideal of Party card, flat, fridge and TV seemed to lack a vital dimension – be it spirituality, political awareness, or faith in culture and tradition.

Yet, on the other side, those who did have higher ideals were possessed with immense creative energy, with a dynamism fed by the country's very diversity, by a faithfulness to traditional roots which avoided the sterile extremes of folklorism and foreign fads. What is more, among intellectuals there was a heady sense of a single community, a community open to any who shared its ideal – even to me, a mere literature student and apprentice translator. This democratic elite – so different from the exclusive and hierarchical cliques of British intellectual life – enabled an enthusiastic cross-fertilisation of art-forms, disciplines and regional cultures. Which in turn helps to explain how postwar Yugoslavia managed to produce a culture out of all proportion to her modest size and material wealth – a Nobel-prize novelist, for instance, world-class poets, a dazzlingly diverse popular music tradition, a unique homegrown school of painting misleadingly called naive.

As for politics, I was touched by the faith, expressed by most I met, in communism as a homegrown revolution, and I shared the universal and genuine admiration for Tito as a wartime and peacetime leader … yet I found the unquestioning nature of this faith oppressive.

There were dissenters, of course. But the consenting relationship between rulers and ruled in Tito's Yugoslavia meant that non-conformers were few, and the forces overseeing conformity – such as the widespread network of Interior Ministry (SUP) informers – were many. Some of those unable to follow the herd retreated into depression. Others quietly held their own, for years dodging incentives and threats to join the Party – for it must be said in fairness that, as secret police went, the Yugoslav SUP were more Balkan than autocratic, preferring to look the other way as long as dissidents didn't make too much noise.

(An endearing memory: Bob and I, walking the Miljačka gorge upriver from Sarajevo, are invited by three men picnicking near the roadside to join their meal: 'Are you on holiday?'

'No we're students at the university. How about you?'

'We're SUP officers, but right now it's our lunch break. Have some more chicken.')

Some political dissent, it is true, had ethnic overtones. The leaders of the Croatian Spring six years before [1971] had been locked up on charges of separatism. The young Hungarians in Novi Sad, my friends from high-school vacations, saw a stealthy Serbianisation going hand-in-hand with attempts at political control (from one of my monthly visits to the next, the Hungarian student café had suddenly become very popular with young Serbian toughs, making free tables hard to find and intimidating to sit at). Nevertheless, the Croats' real crime had been to advocate democratic reform, just as the Hungarians knew full well that covert Serbianisation was not an end in itself, but had the real aim of ensuring political control over a dangerously homogeneous intellectual culture.

Tensions there were; but no worse than the resentments between English, Scots and Welsh back home. Then the Yugoslav system of guaranteed minority rights in local government, education and media terms was upheld – rightly, it seemed – as an example to the world. These guarantees, of course, were a matter of vital necessity in a country made up of a patchwork of minorities – as was shown when they broke down only a couple of years later, with the uprising of the Kosovo Albanians and its murderous repression. This put paid not only to the principle of self-determination of peoples within the Yugoslav federation, but also – by making ethnic hatred a respectable vote-winner – it signalled the bloody downfall of Yugoslavia itself. Then, however, in the late seventies, even the most radical or drunken of dissenters never once questioned in my presence the integrity of Yugoslavia as an amalgam of different peoples, or questioned her borders.

In any case, ethnicity seemed a broad-brush affair, based on language and region rather than ancestry or religion. For the students I knew in Sarajevo, all of whom spoke the Bosnian dialect (about half-way between Serbian and Croatian, but generously spiced with Turkish loan-words), fine ethnic distinctions had little meaning.

Looking back, I can sort Slav from Turkish names, but no further: Snežana, Svetozar; Nermina, Nenad. When I see the ones whose names have faded – the dark-haired, tortoise-shell-spectacled student of English, slinky cabaret singer by night, who took me under her wing; her shy blonde girlfriend, unwitting heartthrob; the languid, penniless poet with ladykilling green eyes and an oft-requited passion for plum brandy, who took over my hostel bed when I left; the glamorous but oh-so-earnest rising Party star – and think of their origins, I draw a blank.

If asked, my friends would have regarded themselves as Yugoslavs.

Perhaps also as Bosnians, though all I recall is normal home-town pride: You must come with me back to Tuzla, to Banja Luka. Ironically, however, what I missed among many of these thoroughly modern young Yugoslavs was a sense of deeper heritage, of faithfulness to traditional roots – little suspecting that history would return not as wisdom, but as vengeance.

A recent simplistic revision of East European history, tarring all communist leaders with Stalin's brush, portrays Tito as an absolute ruler over a misbegotten empire, whose brute force alone kept his citizens from slitting their neighbours' throats. This is a myth; and the fact that former Yugoslavs now spread it (usually to justify the slitting of neighbours' throats) makes it no less of a myth. The cause for the present bloodletting, it seems to me, is rather the opposite. The love for Tito was genuine; but his charisma meant that no questions need ever be asked.

The downfall of the Yugoslav people has been their inability to question the malevolent dictators who followed, preaching not brotherhood and unity but race and blood. Though Tito's Yugoslavia genuinely seemed to have mended the cracks of ancient feud, this, the gap between the complex responsibilities of an exceptionally complex society and simple, charismatic solutions imposed from above, was the fatal faultline it never bridged. When the little Hitlers of today wrenched this gap apart in their lust for power or their fear of the Other, the country shattered along the lines of weakest resistance: religion, language, race. But this is the shape, not the cause, of Yugoslavia's destruction, this land I weep for with her people, this land to which I can never return.

That day, I hunted houses all over the old town, up and down the streets, alleys and stairs that tumbled over the foothills of the Miljačka gorge, which held the city in check to the West. The calm jumble of thick-walled white-washed buildings seemed a continent, a century away from the city below, the sharp smell of diesel, the clang and screech of trams past department stores and offices; and though as old as the Baščaršija at the city's heart, these ancient suburbs had none of its noise and hustle of cafés and souvenir stalls, hawkers and loafers.

And to cap it all, it was suddenly spring; a mild sun had enticed children to play in the street, women in flower-patterned pantaloons to gossip raucously in doorways. Two old men in faded workblue jackets sat side by side, gazing benignly into the middle distance, on a bench by a little triangular graveyard where the turban-capped columns leant higgledy-piggedly and dazzling white in the freshly-washed light.

Golobrdica – bare hillock – was a narrow, cobbled hogback of pantiled single-storey houses and flaking courtyard walls, each one almost as high as the houses it joined. I rang at the roofed gate of number 39, its heavy, nail-bossed door long stripped of paint by rain, frost and sun.

The woman must been in her forties, with sharp, tired eyes and thick brown hair, streaked with grey, pinned up under a floral cotton headscarf; over her brown-and-ochre paisley pantaloons she wore an old green cardigan.

'I've come about the room. For me and my wife.'

She motioned me inside with a downward flick of her hand. Through a tiny whitewashed courtyard and the kitchen, where an old man, big and stooped, watery-eyed and wheezing with asthma, examined me intently as I passed.

The room was a white cell with a single bed, an unvarnished spruce chest, a table and chair, and a little round woodstove painted silver; and though the sun shone in through the small square window in the wall a half-metre thick, it still held the cool of winter.

'I'll take it.'

The other door off the kitchen led into the main room of the house. She motioned me inside: '*Hajde, sjedi.*' (Sit down.)

A divan covered with woven rugs ran round three of the walls; the fourth, windowed, overlooked a steep little valley of backyards: vegetable plots, washing lines, chicken runs, and plum trees, their bare branches speckled dark pink and green with opening blossom. Apart from a low oblong table and a TV set behind the door, there was little furniture; the floor was covered with old, hand-woven kelim carpets in three or four different patterns of maroon, indigo, and green, their colours faded and blended with washing.

The woman returned, bearing a copper tray with a brass and copper *džezva* – the long-handled can, shaped like an inverted cone, for cooking the coffee – and three tiny gold-rimmed porcelain bowls.

'So when is your wife coming?'

'Not for two or three weeks. She's in Holland. I'll write today and tell her I've found somewhere to live.'

The old man nodded, but the woman quickly continued: 'But we want to rent the room right away.'

'That's fine, I can move in this week.'

I handed over the three red hundred-dinar notes; she folded them away in her purse, which she put back in her apron pocket.

Our coffee finished, the landlady took me into the courtyard. Next to the house door was the toilet – instead of paper, a water tap. Then, off the kitchen, the partitioned cubicle with its sitting bath. She hesitated in front of the fridge.

'I could clear you a shelf in here…'

She hesitated again.

'It's just that we don't want anything…dirty in there, you understand?

I didn't understand. There was an awkward silence, until I realised she was talking of pork: 'Oh no don't worry. We don't eat meat at all.' Though her look was as nonplussed as mine a moment before, she nodded, at least somewhat reassured.

Elated, I descended the flight of steps at the end of the narrow street. Ahead the sun, sinking in a clear sky, was almost touching the squat, barrel-shaped minaret of the walled mosque opposite, on the other side of the little built-up valley leading down towards the centre of town. The shadows were suddenly cold, and I realised I had not eaten since the morning.

Down another flight of stairs, and the twin towers of the Catholic cathedral across the road gave me my bearings. Dolphin-nosed, drab-green trucks snarled past with baby Fiats in their wake, their sharp fumes filling the narrow road lined with grimy nineteenth-century buildings. The market had closed for the day. I turned left along the narrow pavement and into the second doorway, as a tram clanged past a metre from my shoulder.

The shop had all the allure of a station washroom: white-tiled, with a light blue formica shelf and mirror along the left-hand wall; at the back, two steps up to a windowless room with four formica tables and cheap wooden chairs. On the right, a marble counter with an enormous set of scales, and a glass cabinet with flat circular tins of *burek*. But oh, what *burek*! Vast coils of brown strudel pastry, warm, crisp, deliciously filling, that oozed melted butter, and sharp sheep's cheese, or fried pumpkin, or spiced apple, or best of all, the *zeljanica* – a savoury, succulent mix of cheese and spinach that was the next best thing to heaven on earth.

Halfway through my second plate, I leaned back in the chair and stretched contentedly. It was good to be back.

Perhaps it is wrong, in these evil days, with Sarajevo under siege, with Bosnia's enemies shelling bread queues and starving her people out of their homes, when our TV sets show us emaciated babies with mouths writhed in a soundless scream, to write of Bosnia as a land of food. But perhaps it is more important to keep faith with memory: not for my sake, but for the sake of a land where memory may soon be all we have to cling to. Invaders down the ages have been drawn to conquest by Bosnia's rich upland pastures and the orchards of her valleys. Other enemies have burnt her fields, have put her villages to the knife or sword and slaughtered her flocks. And yet, fields can be sown again, the blackened plum tree puts forth new shoots, the massacre's cowed survivors come down from their caves and build shacks from the rubble.

But the new overlords are not content with conquest, with subjugation. They mean to obliterate a people; and they know full well that the most effective obliteration comes from within, by setting neighbour against neighbour. But to wipe out a people, it is not enough to harry, to burn and to kill. Memory itself must be cleansed – the memory that there ever was such a land, a land where the living was good, a land that all its people knew as home.

So let these memories exist. The sharp, tangy scent of hot sheep-cheese as a dish of burek is flipped from a wooden oven paddle to cool on the marble slab. A rich, steaming, oily stew, topped with glistening peppers, on a table shaded by the young leaves of a lime tree in a caravanserai courtyard. Bubbly coils of hot doughnut pastry and tangy ewe-milk curds, washed down with the fifth Nikšičko beer of the evening, at the musicians' table of the Hotel Bristol. The scented sepia foam on the coffee in the red-enamel pan that turns cream-coloured as you stir it. Or the cheese market, a vision in white: great porcelain bowls of curd, soft, glistening slabs of new cheese, stacked wet and scented on the long marble counters, in front of the starched aprons and head-dresses of the plump peasant women. And the day the oranges came: after a winter of carrots and cabbage, pickled or green, the market behind the cathedral suddenly a riot of vermilion, miniature suns piled high on every stall, raucously yelling Buy us! Eat us! Gorge yourself on summer!

As I stepped out of the burek shop into the rush-hour street, I knew that I had another pilgrimage to make. Turning left along Marshal Tito Street, I crossed in front of the gated wall that Islamic law had decreed should shield the eyes of the faithful from the Old Orthodox Church behind.

At least the Turks allowed the Christians to build. Though first-class citizenship was reserved as a perk of Islam, the Ottomans were in fact far more tolerant of other faiths than most Christian

states of their era – a philosophy born of pragmatism, for bigotry
makes inefficient politics when it comes to ruling a multinational
state. When the Jews were expelled from Spain in 1492, for instance,
they found refuge in the Ottoman Empire: for four and a half cen-
turies, until the Nazi death camps, Sarajevo was one of Europe's
great Sephardic cities. And if one from a subject people embraced
Islam, non-Turkish origins were no obstacle to the highest offices of
Empire. Such as Gazi Husrev Beg, the sixteenth-century local boy
made good, who invested his home town with buildings worthy of
the Imperial City itself – a university, a covered bazaar. And the
great mosque, to which I was now returning.

In the alley opposite the wall of the church, the souvenir-shop
owners were packing away their copper trays and coffee pots, their
factory-woven celim rugs and peasant slipper pincushions. By the
alley window of the striplight-lit sweetshop down at the corner, a
conscript soldier and his girl were huddled, both hands entwined,
across a little marble table. The lad behind the counter, back turned
to the lovers, sporting the first wisps of a moustache and greasy
black hair under his white cotton cap, was staring out through the
other window into the gathering dusk.

The metal grille in the mosque wall still stood half-open. Inside
was a silence deepened, not broken, by the splash of water. Across
the yard, where the corner of the great mosque almost touched the
courtyard wall, night was already claiming its domain. An old man,
black-capped, the blue of his jacket intense in the half-light, swept
dust very slowly into a long-handled pan. Afraid to disturb the
silence, I sidled to the stone seat beneath the plane tree, perhaps a
lime, whose leaves were beginning to unfold; its smooth white sur-
face was still warm with sun. Water trickled from the brass taps in
the side of the high, octagonal fountain, under the ornate cast-iron
arabesques of its canopy. The portico of the mosque was lost to
shadows, but its arches of carven stone still curved, serene, weight-
less and high. Over the dome, the minaret soared white in the dying
light, a slender starship waiting for flight.

This was the city's still centre, the very essence of Islam: in a
walled courtyard, water, a tree and the warm geometry of stone. In
the deep blue velvet sky by the minaret hung a sliver of incandes-
cent silver light: the first moon of spring.

ABDULAH SIDRAN

Translations by TED HUGHES / ANTONELA GLAVINIĆ
and JOHN HARTLEY WILLIAMS

Abdulah Sidran was born in 1944 in Binjezevo, near Sarajevo, and studied literature at Sarajevo University. The recipient of many awards for his poetry, he is also a noted scriptwriter, and wrote the screenplays for Emir Kusturica's *Do You Remember Dolly Belle?* and *When Father Was Away on Business.* A poet rich in the dramatics of verbal tone, Sidran blends an intense interest in Sarajevo – in one poem, he calls himself 'the sick man of Sarajevo' – with a poetry of oriental charm. Melancholy and suffering radiate from his evocation of vanished worlds. He continues to live in Sarajevo, where he remained throughout the siege.

Main publications: *Šahbaza* (1970), *Bone and Flesh* (1976), *Sarajevo Collection* (1979), *Selected Poems* (1987), *Sarajevo Tabut* (1995, translated into French as *Je suis une île au coeur du monde*).

Gavrilo

The night is unreal, quiet, like hell –
Which does not exist. The world,
Its houses, its clutter, lies
Deep in oil. This is the moment for you,
The hesitant one, the undecided, to go
Down that rotten stair, your hand
Feeling for that wall, touching the oil,
Saying: Come on, my heart, let's get the weapons! Because

The night is so unreal –
And far too quiet. And there is no one
To tell us: Tomorrow, for you – horror.
Tomorrow, for you – love. The skull fills
With a terrible brightness. Hurry, hurry, the weapons –
Before the bone splits in the glare.
Somewhere close they are forging a shield – a true

And real shield, and this darkness
Embroiders for you, my heart, a warm cloak,
For you, everything, my shaking heart. We have to
Hurry, before the bone cracks, and dawn comes
Bursting our ear-drums with the screams from the street
And we suck in air mixed with hot shrapnel.

Gavrilo Princep: One of the assassins of Archduke Ferdinand and his wife.

Hurry, hurry, my heart, get the weapons, before it dawns –
Before our god dies. Afterwards
There will be nobody to talk to
And nothing to talk with.
We'll be lying dead under the oil
In darkness – under the deaf
Heavy blunt years that press down
On this century's shoulders as this night
So unreal so overfull of brightness
Presses on my shoulders – crying Hurry
Hurry, my heart, let's get the weapons!

[TH/AG]

A Dispute About God

I

The other day some serious people remarked:
there is no God. Silence fell for thousands and thousands

of years, none of which lasted for one moment
longer than a moment. Then, heard

in that silence, some kind of, like, music
came from somewhere – so that nothing else could be heard!

Someone with a good ear – no one special,
which was why he heard it – swore blind, while

his face shivered with laughter, he'd caught
in that silence, in that music, a whisper completely

human, except it had sounded not as if
it came from a human throat – but God's.

II

So how about that, then? No God?
I've always been able to think or dream

anything I've a mind to, but an absence like that,
in a thought or a dream, would never have

occurred to me! Things confirm already
some kind of presence, don't they? To count

how many Gods there are, what amount
exactly, you need no special skills. So,

if you'll allow me, there are at least two versions
we have to consider: one, there are as many

Gods as there are people, and two,
which simplifies the matter somewhat,

there are actually two: one who exists and gives,
and one who doesn't and therefore doesn't give.

As you can see – we're not building castles
in the air – there are two versions and neither

starts from nowhere!

III

Do you suppose it's God who's been
selling you – and for how many millennia? –

short on the truth? You can see him, but
he doesn't exist. He simply doesn't want to know

you. Or put in an appearance. He's a no show
who groans and lurches and dies miserably

on wasteground, between churches. (Telling
these apart, by their insides or outsides,

would be an utter waste of time, you'd really
need to want to do it.) Besides,

he doesn't exist. Don't look for his house, his roof
(no chimney, no smoke), give up, abandon your search,

for the conceivable. Or, if you must – take a look
around you: he's there, in everything, unseizable.

IV

What follows threw us into something like confusion.
Needing to start with something other than illusion,

we reached for certainty. So. In the beginning was The Word.
Hills bulged, waters swam around aimlessly,

for a long while flora hesitated, fauna even longer! Nobody
saw it, but there are stories, how from everywhere music

floated out. Clearly the player knew why he did
what there was to do. Music got to know the world,

and *vice versa.* The plants got cracking. Birds flew.
Beasts made a racket! (Plant power was proof

of something, too.) Let there be fish, beasts and birds –
and there they were! The skies spread

everywhere, and everywhere the word rolled. It was
only after that – and just in time – that man came

and firmly grasped the word. Carved roads. Tamed
hills and water. By tasting everything around with earth-

embracing notions, made countless tongues. Vessels
that sailed, then flew. Created various mighty senses.

So why scold or criticise the One Who Exists in skies?
Who subsists in beasts, clouds and breasts. Who Exists.

V

This isn't a matter where one can say: Look! There!
Some of it, obviously, you just offer up

like a prayer. What's clear at the moment is
that there was music, that it's lasted till now,

that it doesn't matter whether a player played it,
or whether it played itself, that it's still

playing, and that at least two gods exist: The One
Who Does and the one who doesn't. No point

wasting more words on the latter: he's both here
and not here, neither causing nor healing disease.

And not much about the former, either, except
he definitely exists. He appears in dreams, not

like a man but like a word spoken by a glistening
velvet voice. *'I exist. I am. Let your soul be pure.'*

'Let your soul be pure. I exist. I am.'
Showing himself thus, by means of dreams, He

manages to make me not exist, as if I'd never been,
and then to be again, like always, the same bone, the same

meat in the same parcel of skin, assembled from the
same pain. Turning night to day, He makes me see

everything, even my own death, how and why
it will happen. For the hundredth time, I wake

at twenty to three in my ripped bed, soaked in sweat
and collect my thoughts for the hundredth time. Sidran?

Is this you? Is this your bed? When all the ships
sink, when the world totters and falls, He is the one

who stays close to your soul. He exists – how much
of him there is! – in a poet's fingers, scribbling

a song, everywhere, always, here and now! He's not
substance, not even a symbol. And yet He is, helping me

skilfully, ever more skilfully, to bear the pain of being,
leading me lamb-like, gently, toward the end of being.

[JHW]

Into the Great Mist

Listen: how quietly
The tired Earth's hair is turning grey.
The World decamps into the great mist.

This island, this razed field, sinks away.

And when they are sunk
And changed into the slow seeds
These heads of ours will be swayed for a long time
By a thick wind, underground.

Only the words will survive –
Those words we never uttered –
And because of them (this is the marvel)
Our existence here will be long remembered.

Listen: how quietly
the tired Earth's hair is turning grey.
The World decamps into the great mist.

[TH/AG]

Those Who Cross

To begin with, time passed.
We crossed the bridge and the road by
the petrol station, and there
reasonably enough it said: NO SMOKING,
so we crossed the road again, with
hesitant steps, under Trebević, fearing
change, a sudden shower.

> Dead air. A stone. A snake.
> The frozen chlorophyll of Toledo.
> *Españoles sin patria.*

Afterwards, time passed. We looked
one another in the eyes, summing it up for
the thousandth time. How shall we root out
the heart of this sadness? Someone
had left us. Yahweh will be alone again.

ombre prejado y entelegente
lavrador publico dija i tarde

Then time passed. We climbed
the stairway, not counting the steps, to the stone
quadrature (here lies the one who has departed)
Jasenovac, Gradiška, Djakovo, Jadovono,
Loborgrad, Auschwitz, Bergen-Belsen, peace.

Clara, no lloras hija mia,
no temes la fosa fria.

And further time passed. Down below,
was dona Clara in a bikini, the marks of indolence
strewn around her head: *die Sonnenbrille*, 'ELLE',
and there a *Feuerzeug*, cigarettes, a little music box
from Japan. A heart has stopped beating.

Muy presto te perdimos
caro padre amoroso
yece con nuesta madre
en eterno reposo.

The world's a torch, burning
at both ends. Thus we are alone – the living, the dead –
always the same. Is Elohim crying?
Adonai whimpering? Here, for a long time, no one
has cut the grass or the weeds. Only the lindens flower
and the walnut ripens. The earth is clean, unblemished.

Madre que non conoce otra justicia
que el perdon ni mas ley que amor.

You who have crossed that final
highway, sleep. Let time go by. Sleep,
and time will cease. Sleep, for nothing

will be and nothing will ever have been.
Sleep, for the sky remembers nothing. There is only
Nothing, a black hole. Nothing Which Flows
To A Black Hole
Which
Grows

[JHW]

NOTES:

Those who cross: the name *Hebrew* is said to derive from *ebher*, beyond, or
abhar, to cross over. On the expulsion of the Jews from Spain in 1492, many
'españoles sin patria' (Spaniards without a homeland) found refuge in the cities
of the Ottoman Empire.
Ombre prejado...: An esteemed and intelligent man, public worker by day and
night.
Clara, no lloras...: Clara, do not weep, my daughter, do not fear the cold grave.
Muy presto te perdismo...: We lost you very early, dear loving father; lie with
our mother in eternal rest.
Thus, quick and dead, are we all alone: Epitaph on the grave of Elias Kabilje
in Sarajevo's Jewish cemetery.
Madre que non conoce...: Mother who knew no other justice than pardon and
no other law than love.

The Partisan Cemetery

We'll take a little stroll out of town,
Give the soul a rest. On a walk
Thinking becomes crystalline, it seems
We see things as they are: this
Is a path lined with trees, these
Are the green blouses of chestnuts
Opening above us, young and tender
Lovers murmur around us. This is day-time.
This is the light
Breaking wisely among the leaves, resting on the marble
Above the road, and on the cemetery
Where we too rest briefly. Tell me,
My dear little sister, can you imagine yourself
In some other person's memory? The rain

Has washed off the lettering, but
Bring your ear closer. That whistling
Whisper is the subterranean
Soul of water, it is the earth
Eating bone – whereby history
And harmony unfold
Only for an instant among us, for us
Only a momentary flicker.
Then without us, without us,
And without us. The planet
Goes on breathing, the child's eyes grow wider,
An apple still breaks open in
The kiss of a little girl.
A bird flies over. Lamentation
Has no place here. This is no time
For wailing. The dead
Are here simply to set our sufferings
In perspective. So now let's go – slowly
As after a feast, a wholly Slavonic
Feast in a graveyard, souls intoxicated.
Let the bone walk, the flesh
Walk. The books, little sister, are open –
The history is being written.
The Martyrology is open. What remains
For us
Is to remember our names, and never to forget them,
Never, never again, to forget them.

[TH/AG]

A Blind Man Sings to His City

The rain stops. Now from the drains,
From the attics, from under the floorboards
Of the shattered homes in the suburbs
Oozes the stench of the corpses
Of mice. I walk seeking
No special meaning in this. A blind man,
To whom it has been given to see

Only what others don't. This
Makes up for my deprivation: in the south wind
That touches me I recognise the voices
Of those who left this city. As if they were crying.
There, scent of the linden trees, close.
I know
The bridge is near, where my step and my stick
Will ring differently – more light
In the sound. There, now, right by my ear
Two flies mate in the air.
It will be scorching hot again. Bodies
Brush past me, hot,
Smelling of bed, smelling of lust. I walk muttering
To God, as if He were beside me:
'Surely nobody knows this city
Better than me – better than me, God,
To whom you have given never to see
The face he loves.'

[TH/AG]

Chronicle of a Miracle
'I have never seen anything for the first time.'

With your left hand
You push a thick mass of hair back from your forehead and
As your hand moves I have shifted
That gesture into memory and already
No longer see you push hair with hand from forehead
But am remembering how with your left hand
You push a thick mass of hair back from your forehead

You say with a voice that trembles
And stirs the candle-flame on the table in front of us
'It's stormy outside' and something not me but
Where there is some part of me (and what a part)
Shifts that voice into memory so that I am not
Only listening to you I am remembering
Listening to you and remembering your voice

That trembles and stirs the candle-flame on the table
In front of us and remembering
The evening and the voice saying 'It's stormy outside'

And it goes on being stormy outside and the evening
Goes on just as the life goes on which
No I don't seem to be living only remembering
Like the voice with which you are still saying
'It's stormy outside' the voice I remember like
The hand with which you push a mass of hair back from your forehead
As you speak the hand I remember, touching it
For the first time

[TH/AG]

Sarajevo sings

Immense is the Earth. Continents
Drift and adversity
Heaves up everywhere, but this is
Different. The forest in the North
And the forest in the South smell the same.
And that smell resembles nothing
Man has ever heard, seen, touched.
He widens his nostrils in vain (did Mama's
Womb smell like that to the embryo?)
It's the smell of nothing singing
And sobbing with the same voice.
And love and misery here
Wear the same face. Everything is the same.
At the gates the guards overcome
By horror dream on their feet (Flight, soft
Non-existent wing!) but the same
Voice will shake them from their sleep:
'Sarajevo, may the lightning roast you!'
It's somebody
Yelling for my help again. The sage
And the desperate, the child, the derelict, the scoundrel –
Before my face, all equal. Everything,

Here, is the same, equal. I am an island
In the heart of the world and nothing
Reaches me. Nothing but the torpid
Blood and the shudder going though it.
A silence, surrounded by nothing.

[TH/AG]

Why Venice Is Sinking

I look at the sky over Venice.
Nothing's changed for the last
seven billion years. God's up there. He
created the universe and then
the seven billion worlds in it
and in every world innumerable nations,
a babel of tongues, but only one Venice.

He made each nation different, whispering: 'Now
get acquainted.' He gave them foreign languages
to get better acquainted with, making them all,
by this means, richer and better. He made
Venice the way he did birds and fish, just like that, so
people and nations would come to believe in him,
being, of course, thunderstruck by what he could do.

I look at the sky over Venice. Up there and everywhere –
is God. The only one. He created the universe,
seven billion worlds in the universe, and every world
filled with people and languages, to which he added
a single Venice. And on one world, upon a landmass known
as Europe, among the tribe of the southern slavs, he placed
a small addenda. This is the border. *Bosnia. Bos-
nia. Bosnia.* And here the Eastern cross
and the Western cross, formed of one cross, met
and went to war. But the Bosnians, being meek,
took a third faith and hewed to the unique God,
the only One, neither begotten, nor himself a begetter,
Lord of the world, the Master of Judgement Day.

I look at the sky over Venice. Worldly rulers
have decided that Bosnians should be – nowhere.
Venice is sinking. Europe is sinking. The cradle is sinking
and children in their cradles are sinking. Continents are sinking.
Roses in Murano glass vases are sinking. Murano
is sinking. Hotel rooms are sinking and
the Dead Poets Society is sinking. Why doesn't the world need
Bosnians? Amongst colours – one colour less?
Amongst scents – one scent less? Why doesn't the world need
Venice? Amongst wonders – one wonder less?

I look at the sky over this earthly world.
In a long arc, a single star is breaking up, right down
through the bottomless universe, falling, it seems,
right into the Grand Canal. This ordinary world, among
seven billion celestial worlds, is about to become poorer
by a whole people. Its worldly rulers appear to have
so decided. In the universe, therefore, a single falling star.
And Venice is sinking. The universe will be poorer
by a whole world. That is the will of the Lord of worlds,
the will of the Master of Judgement Day.

[JHW]

IZET SARAJLIĆ

Translations by CHARLES SIMIC

Izet Sarajlić was born in 1930 in Doboj, grew up in Trebinje, Herzegovina, and studied Philosophy at the University of Sarajevo. Since 1945 he has lived in Sarajevo, where he remained (and was wounded by a shell) during the siege. The grace, transparency and precision of his poems stem from his desire for his poetry to communicate effectively when read in public. He worked as a journalist and an editor in a publishing house, and in 1971 became the president of the Writers Union of Bosnia-Herzegovina; but was dismissed seventeen days later and, subsequently, expelled from the Communist Party. He has received numerous prizes for his poetry, and was one of the most popular and widely translated writers of the former Yugoslavia. His translators have included Joseph Brodsky, Hans Magnus Enzensberger and Yevgeni Yevtushenko.

Main publications: *Encounter* (1945), *Grey Weekend* (1955), *A Moment of Silence* (1960), *Dedication* (1961), *Transit* (1963), *Intermezzo* (1965), *The Wilson Promenade* (1969), *Letters* (1974), *The Thirteenth Chapbook of Poems* (1978), *Necrology for a Nightingale* (1987), *Selected Works* (1990), and *Sarajevo War Collection* (1992).

My Sojourn in Istanbul

There are several versions
of my sojourn in Istanbul.

According to one,
It was a sojourn of suspicious political nature.

According to another one,
it had to do with one of my sentimental novels.

In the third version,
even the selling of drugs is mentioned.

The fact that I've never been to Istanbul
did not interest anyone, of course.

The Criticism of Poetry

Why is it that the critics of poetry
do not write poetry
when they know so much about it?

If they did really know,
most likely they'd write poems
rather than write about them.

Critics of poetry are like old men
who know everything about love
except they do not know how to make love.

The Blues

It would be interesting to know
what will happen to our souls after our deaths?

It will be interesting to know
will our souls get wet in the rain after our deaths?

It would be interesting to know
if our souls will still rush toward each other
      after our deaths?

It would be interesting to know
what our souls will feel when spring comes
      after our deaths?

It would be interesting to know
how our souls will talk to each other without our eyes?

Untitled

If I had died that Friday in Paris
who would have sent a telegram that I'm no more
when it would have taken three days
to convince the police that I existed at all.

If that Saturday I had died in Warsaw,
a beautiful lady would have lost her job,
a beautiful lady from the Polish Writers Union
in whose care my soul was entrusted.

If I had died that Sunday in Leningrad,
it would have been even worse.
The white night would have worn a black band
        on its sleeve.
Now tell me, what kind of white night would that be
        with a black band on its sleeve?

If that Tuesday I had died in Berlin,
Neues Deutschland would announce that a Yugoslav
writer of the middle generation
suddenly died of a heart attack, while I – and this is
        not just idle talk –
need to croak on my native soil.

You see how good it is that I didn't die,
        and that I'm once again among you?
You can whistle, you can applaud.
You see how good it is that I didn't die,
and that I'm once again among you all.

Luck in Sarajevo

In Sarajevo
in the spring of 1992,
everything is possible:
you go stand in a bread line
and end up in an emergency room
with your leg amputated.

Afterwards, you still maintain
that you were very lucky.

In the Evening

On the soccer field
a young man
plays the guitar
while over his head
a grenade
flies from Poljana.

Is he Sarajevo's future
Bulat Okudzava?

Young man,
just stay alive,

art, which meant everything
to me once,
art is, believe me,
truly of no importance.

Softly with a Touch of Sadness

The rain like a forgotten march beating against the windows.
It's fall again; the classic season of elegies.
I'll drop by the train station to accustom myself to parting.
If I don't return, my poems will remain to roam this city.
Once there was youth in the already ancient yesterday,
In your heart and mine, there was, is, and will be.
I'm leaving, but someone else resembling me
will perhaps visit the graves of the fallen instead of me
to study the syntax of absence.
My poems will always come handy to them.

It's time, I'm going. I represent the past, you said.
Greetings to everything new that came with
a greater, more tender love.
No one can anymore call me snot-nose,
that privileged and honorary name,
as if one were saying: spring.

How I envy that snot-nose Izet Sarajlić from the VII A.
who in the inherited military overcoat
unaware of the wrong use of the over-used verb love
is starting out to conquer the world.
I will never again be able to write my first elegy.
I will never again be seventeen years old,
nor twenty five.

I'm going. Already? Shall I be just a memory?
There's still so much I wanted to say.
I'm going. I'm still here. If you stop by Tvrtkova 9/3,
I'll treat you to tea and memories.
I'm still here. A minute of silence for me.

DARA SEKULIĆ

Translations by CHARLES SIMIC

Dara Sekulić was born in 1931 in Kordunski Ljeskovac, near Banja Luka, and lived in Sarajevo from 1953 until her departure during the war. She trained as a social worker and worked for *Oslobodjenje* (*Liberation*), Sarajevo's daily, for many years. A recipient of several major literary awards, her poetry is distinguished by great lyrical concentration and intensity, in which the solitary voice speaks out from a world in which tragedy and injustice loom. She is, writes Charles Simic, 'a poet both intimate and metaphysical in ways that remind me of Emily Dickinson and Paul Celan'. She is now based at the Heinrich Böll Institute in Germany.

Main publications: *Poems* (1956), *A Dreamed Home* (1958), *Reckless* (1963), *Bitter Inn* (1970), *Close Pulse* (1975), *With a Face Towards the Earth* (1978), *Selected Poems* (1985), and *The Wasteland Spirit* (1990).

Ave Maria

Crusaders pierced your maidenhead with daggers
and pale sleepwalkers with their prayers,
bad-tempered and tall, hairy talkative ones,
and the quiet, warped ones full of poison,
and the irresistible, lethargic Don Juans,
oh my God, oh my Maria,
in how many foul beds
you sowed your holy scent?

Greetings to you. No one had charity and pity for you.
With a cut-throat look they charged at you.
While I sob, I sadly think of myself too.
They called you a well-bred lady
and all at least once knelt before you.
And afterwards, in taverns, called you
a cheap slut who pretends to be a saint.

Oh Maria my bitter halo,
put out with shame in daylight
and lit in faith at dusk.

Your lips thirst the hush of a gentle touch;
cowards raped you, made your arms heavy.

They all had you, and you never had anyone,
no one ever touched you.
That's how you took the Holy Ghost into your womb.

In your fall and misery
every one spoke of you reverently,
implored you in God's name,
and hinted at a liaison with some fellow.
Everyone asked you to pray for them.

On your knees you extolled them
with your kindness,
oh poor Maria,
this is my own prayer for you.

Tomb

Gather your red hair,
the ants have recognised you.
How long can forgetting last?
Let love find you neat and tidy
when it appears. You are a woman.
Any minute now it'll come to you.

Move, stretch your arm,
already your elbows and fingernails
draw the world's breath
out of the cracks in the false balsam.
Everything is within the reach of truth:
voices, letters, hairpins.

Tenderly they took leave of you,
from nowhere to never travelling,
they pictured empty chambers
over your face, sweets and grains
and aromatic pots by your side
to minister to you.

Up to your windows the green stalks reach,
in exile adjourned
the Queen turns mouldy.
Even your crown has darkened.
The time for you always inopportune,
gray love never to happen.

The Breakfast of the Blind

The hand lights the way for morsels
lifted from the plate into the mouth.
All the sweetness of the morning,
the warmth of the coming day,
milky delight over the bent backs
and colours of a hot breakfast
pucker softly in each adam's apple.

The blind do not finish their meals.
The morsels grow weary in their fingers
as their faces begin to see –
without seeing the play of spilled crumbs
over the dishes and table-ends.

For them, the morning is the scent
of something evaporating, like a ball of twine
unwound from the dark corner,
the one seen in a nightmare.
And breakfast lengthens like a warm spiderweb.

The blind have no hunger in their eyes.

Lament

Where I come from giving birth meant nothing.
I can't remember the names of all my younger brothers.

You were like the earth itself.
Perhaps that's why your lap was so warm.

Every fall your white peasant skirt
turned red after giving birth.

What colour was your hair?
Your black kerchief made me think of bread.

If I knew where you were buried,
I'd make the springs of the earth weep.

Danilo Kiš (1935-1989) was born in Subotica, Vojvodina (a province of Serbia, formerly autonomous) to a Hungarian Jewish father and a Montenegrin mother. His father and almost all his family were murdered in Auschwitz. By the time of his own death in Paris, he was the best-known Yugoslav writer. His major works of fiction, which include *Garden, Ashes, A Tomb for Boris Davidović, Hourglass, The Encyclopaedia of the Dead*, have been translated widely. This brief text quickly became the focus of much controversy. Kiš himself, relishing the scandal it provoked, called it 'notorious'.

Hubert Butler (1900 -1991) is modern Ireland's most distinguished essayist. He lived in Zagreb for three years in the mid-thirties and wrote frequently about Yugoslavia. Four volumes of his essays were published in Ireland in the 80s and early 90s, and a selected volume of his work, *The Sub-Prefect Should Have Held His Tongue*, was published by Penguin in 1992.

DANILO KIŠ

On Nationalism (1973)

Translated by IVANA DJORDJEVIĆ

Nationalism is first and foremost paranoia. Collective and individual paranoia. As collective paranoia it results from envy and fear, and most of all from the loss of individual consciousness; this collective paranoia is therefore simply an accumulation of individual paranoias at the pitch of paroxysm. If, in the framework of a social order, an individual is not able to "express himself", because the order in question is not congenial and does not stimulate him as an *individual*, or because it thwarts him as an individual, in other words does not allow him to assume an entity of his own, he is obliged to search for this entity outside identity and outside the so-called social structure. Thus he becomes a member of a pseudo-masonic group which seems to pose problems of epochal importance as its goals and objectives: the survival and prestige of a nation or nations, the preservation of tradition and the nation's sacrosanct values – folkloric, philosophical, ethical, literary, etc. Invested with such a secret, semi-public, or public mission, A.N. Other becomes a man of action, a tribune of the people, a semblance of an individual. Once we have him cut down to size, isolated from the herd, and out of the pseudo-masonic lodge where he had installed himself or been installed by others, we are faced with an individual without individuality, a nationalist, Cousin Jules. This the Jules that Sartre wrote about, a zero in his family, a man whose only distinction is that he can blanch at the mere mention of a single topic: the English. This pallor, this trembling, this 'secret' – to be able to blanch at the mention of the English – constitute his social being and make him important, existent: do not mention *English* tea in front of him, or the others will start winking and signalling, kicking you under the table, because Jules is touchy about the English (and loves his own fold, the French), in a word, Jules is a personality, becomes a personality, thanks to *English* tea. This kind of profile, which fits all nationalists, can be freely elaborated to its conclusion: the nationalist is, as a rule, equally piffling as a social being and as an individual. Outside the commitment he has made, he is a nonentity.

He neglects his family, his job (usually in an office), literature (if he is a writer), his social responsibilities, since these are all petty compared with his messianism. Needless to say, he is *by choice* an ascetic, a potential fighter biding his time. Paraphrasing Sartre on anti-Semitism, nationalism is a comprehensive and free choice, a global attitude not only toward other nations but toward people in general, toward history and society; it is at once a passion and a worldview. The nationalist is by definition an ignoramus. Nationalism is the line of least resistance, the easy way. The nationalist is untroubled, he knows or thinks he knows what his values are, his, that's to say national, that's to say the values of the nation he belongs to, ethical and political; he is not interested in others, *they are no concern of his*, hell – it's other people (other nations, another tribe). They don't even need investigating. The nationalist sees other people in his own image – as nationalists. A comfortable standpoint, as we noted. Fear and envy. A commitment and engagement needing no effort. Not only is hell other people, in a national key of course, but also: whatever is not mine (Serbian, Croatian, French…) is alien to me.

Nationalism is an ideology of banality. As such, nationalism is a totalitarian ideology. Nationalism is moreover, and not only in the etymological sense, the last remaining ideology and demagogy that addresses itself to the *people*. Writers know this best. That's why every writer who declares that he writes 'about the people and for the people', who claims to surrender his individual voice to the *higher* interests of the nation, should be suspected of nationalism. Nationalism is also kitsch: in its Serbo-Croatian variant it takes the form of squabbling about the national origin of GINGERBREAD HEARTS.*

As a rule the nationalist doesn't know a single foreign language or any variant of his own, nor is he familiar with other cultures (they are no concern of his). But there is more to it than this. If he does know foreign languages, which means that as an intellectual he has an insight into the cultural heritage of other nations, great or small, they serve only to let him draw analogies, to the detriment of those others, naturally. Kitsch and folklore, folkloric kitsch if you prefer, are nothing but camouflaged nationalism, a fertile field for nationalist ideology. The upsurge of folklore studies, both in this country and in the world at large, is due to nationalism, not anthropology. Insisting on the famous *couleur locale* is likewise, outside an artistic context (i.e., unless in the service of artistic truth), a covert form of nationalism. Nationalism is thus, in the first place, negativity; nationalism is a negative spiritual category because it thrives on denial and by denial. We are not what they are. We are the positive pole, they the negative. Our values, national, nationalist, have no function except in relation to the nationalism of those

---

* Biscuits in the shape of hearts, or people, or things, decorated with coloured sugar, and sold by bakers in Vojvodina, Serbia, and other parts of ex-Yugoslavia.

others: we are nationalist, but they are even more so; we slit throats (when we must) but they do too and even more; we are drunkards, they are alcoholics; our history is proper only *in relation* to theirs; our language is pure only *in relation* to theirs. Nationalism lives by relativism. There are no general values – aesthetic, ethical, etc. Only relative ones. And it is principally in this sense that nationalism is reactionary. *All* that matters is to be better than my brother or half-brother, the rest is no concern of mine. To jump not very high but higher than him; the others do not count. This is what we have defined as fear. Others are allowed to catch us up, even to overtake us; that is no concern of ours. The goals of nationalism are always attainable, *attainable* because modest, modest because mean. You don't go jumping or shot-putting to reach *your* own best but to beat the only others who matter, so similar and so different, on whose account you took the field. The nationalist, as we noted, fears no one but his brother. But him he fears with an existential, pathological dread; for the *chosen* enemy's victory is his own *total* defeat, the annihilation of his very being. As a shirker and a nonentity the nationalist does not aim high. Victory over the chosen enemy, the other, is total victory. This is why victory, victory that is guaranteed and defeat that is never final. The nationalist fears no one, 'no one save God', but his God is made to his own measure, it is his double sitting at the next table, his own entity, the conscious and organised section of the family and the nation – pale Cousin *Jim*. To be a nationalist is therefore to be an individual with no obligations. It is to be 'a coward who will not admit his cowardice; a murderer who represses his murderous proclivities without being able to master them, yet who dares not kill except in effigy, or in the anonymity of a crowd; a malcontent who, fearing the consequences of rebellion, dares not rebel' – the spitting image of Sartre's anti-Semite. Whence, we wonder, such cowardice, such an attitude, such an upsurge of nationalism, in this day and age? Oppressed by ideologies, on the margin of social changes, crammed and lost between antagonistic ideologies, unequal to individual rebellion because it is denied to him, the individual finds himself in a quandary, a vacuum; although he is a social being, he takes no part in social life; although he is an individualist, individuality has been refused him in the name of ideology; what is left but to seek his social being *elsewhere*? The nationalist is a frustrated individualist, nationalism is the frustrated (collective) expression of this kind of individualism, at once ideology and anti-ideology...

HUBERT BUTLER

FROM Mr Pfeffer of Sarajevo (1956)

The Sarajevo conspirators* were Croats, Serbs and Moslems, and they aimed at a nation in which the diverse peoples of Yugoslavia should live in free and equal union. They were mostly republicans, and the movement to which they belonged was not tainted with racialism till the new state was set up under the Serbian king. It was racialism, not nationalism, that undermined Yugoslav unity, but this vital distinction is seldom observed and when "petty nationalism" is attacked as the source of our troubles, the "petty nations" seldom defend themselves. Unlike monarchies, empires and Communist states, they have no trade union nor have they developed a common philosophy. They have few arguments to oppose to the universalists and imperialists, who believe that incompatibilities of language and culture are best ironed out by the kindly pressure of a dominant race. In fact, the small peoples often subscribe to this belief themselves. Frequently you will hear an Irish nationalist lamenting the collapse of Austria-Hungary and explaining that Yugoslavia and the other succession states were mere puppet contrivances of the League of Nations, ragbags of racial oddments, doomed to disintegrate. He ignores that these states all have living languages and often a more distinctive culture, a longer history of independence than our own. And since the succession states owed their existence to England and France, their citizens often scoffed at Ireland's independence. The Croats used to call themselves 'the Ulster of Yugoslavia' because they considered the Six Counties as progressive as themselves and in equal danger of being absorbed into the peasant economy of a more primitive people.

What then is nationalism and how can it be distinguished from racialism? Thomas Davis, being only half Irish, is probably a sounder nationalist, more immune from racialism, than Mazzini and the other Victorian apostles of the resurgent peoples. He would have said that a country belongs to the people who were born in it and intend to die there and who make its welfare their chief concern. There is no mention of 'minority rights', because these were assumed. Even in Ireland not many think like that now. Read the speeches reported in the press. Where one man talks of national unity, a hundred will talk of some unity that is racial, confessional or political.

* The assassins of Archduke Ferdinand and his wife in 1914.
† Edward Beneš, president of Czechoslovakia, 1936-38, who resigned after the Munich agreement that validated Germany's occupation of his country.

It was because nationalism lacked a philosophy that in the early 1920s it began to decay and racialism took its place. The first sign of this degeneration came in 1923, when by the Treaty of Lausanne in exchange for Turks from Europe over a million Greeks were moved from the coast of Asia Minor, where they had lived for three thousand years. This ghastly crime was committed so efficiently under the auspices of the League of Nations that it won universal applause. What Churchill was later to call 'the disentanglement of populations' began to seem a sensible and modern way of solving finally an ancient problem.

The old view that men should enjoy equal rights in the land of their birth began to seem hopelessly out of date, and soon Hitler and Mussolini and Stalin were eliminating causes of friction by large and admirably organised population exchanges in the Tyrol and the Baltic states. The war had hardly started when it became obvious to all sensible Germans that, if there was ever to be world peace, all conquered peoples should be either Germanised or deported. That much-respected man Dr Oberlander, who later became Adenauer's Minister for Refugees, said with reference to the Poles, 'It is better to be harsh now than have petty warfare waged for generations'. Soon the contagion of this generous realism reached the Allies, and in 1940 we find Beneš † writing in *The Nineteenth Century* that 3 million Sudeten Germans should be 'amicably and under decent human conditions' expelled. When the time came they were expelled. Again, Churchill in 1944 expressed the opinion that expulsion was 'the most lasting and satisfactory method' of dealing with the 7.5 million Germans of the east. They, too, were satisfactorily expelled.

When we recall such gigantic endeavours, scientifically conducted, to sort out the old ragbag nations of 1918 into homogeneous states, how petty and parochial seem the dreams of the Sarajevo conspirators, and the poor old League of Nations with its condominiums and Free Cities and minority rights! And how more than dead are Davis and Herder and their romantic insistence on Homeland and Nationhood! One has to listen hard to catch the least echo of that extinct ideology. Yet here is one from the most improbable source of all, from Germany, which once led the world in the social science of Disentanglement. It comes from the Exiles' Charter, an appeal for *Heimatrecht* published on behalf of those 7.5 million German refugees from the east.

> God placed men in their homes. To drive men out of their homes spells spiritual death. We have experienced this fate. Hence we feel called upon to demand that the right to one's home be recognised as one of the basic rights given by God to man.

SEMEZDIN MEHMEDINOVIĆ

A Small Map of the World (1994)

Translated by AMMIEL ALCALAY

The war started on Sunday. I know this because we always played soccer at Skenderija on Sunday. A guy from my team didn't show up that night but no one paid much attention to it. After the game we went out, as always, for a beer. When it came time for the last trolley, I headed home. It happened to be a short ride because a bunch of guys with stockings over their heads and Kalashnikovs aimed at us stopped the trolley. As I got out, I took a look at this crew and recognised the guy from my soccer team who hadn't shown up. I was so taken by surprise that I had to repeat my question twice: 'Sljuka, is that you? Sljuka, is that you?' Embarrassed, he kept quiet behind his stocking.

My confusion lasted for a while. Instead of a guy I was supposed to hang out with over a few beers after a game, I found myself facing a real terrorist occupying the very trolley I happened to be riding in. I couldn't figure out how to explain this to myself, this fundamental physiognomic change. But when the number of people began to multiply – the number of people who, like Sljuka, started wearing stockings on their heads instead of their feet – I was no longer confused.

The next day after the trolley incident, I heard Radovan Karadžić on the news. Every now and then his voice came from off-camera as the screen filled with scenes from the previous day, among them a shot of the gang with stockings over their heads standing in front of the halted trolley. Karadžić spouted such blatant lies that, in a rage, I found a book of his children's poems, *There Are Miracles, There Are No Miracles*, and began ripping it apart. My son, who liked the book, protested so much – he actually threw a fit, even though he himself was scared watching the news – that I stopped, somewhat bewildered. I started taping together the ripped pages to calm down a little boy whose world was being destroyed by grown-ups, a fact he refused to acknowledge. My son knew the author of this book, and he couldn't let himself believe such a man would want to harm him.

I knew him too. He wrote poems that no one in our crowd really thought much of. I certainly didn't. Having faith in my son's taste, however, I had to give my nod of approval to his poetry for children. Karadžić himself was quite aware of the fact that no one thought he had much talent as a writer, but in meeting him it wasn't easy to detect bitterness or, for that matter, the kind of vanity writers usually possess. On the contrary, in all of our meetings he seemed to present reasonable suggestions. He seldom spoke when we hung out in a group at cafés; he just listened. When he did join in to a conversation, his words were calm and reassuring, perhaps because of his years as a psychiatrist. But no one remembered Radovan Karadžić's poems, and the hatred so evident in his early poetry just slipped by. His lines 'Take no pity let's go / kill that scum in the city' would later become a slogan for the war project. Karadžić came across as a peace-loving and good-natured fellow. During the first multi-party elections, after the fall of socialism, he founded the Greens. That seemed quite in character. Founding such a party, given conditions in the Balkans, was more like an artistic performance than true political engagement. The Greens' first action in Sarajevo proved this: They draped plastic bags in various colours over the boughs of the acacias lining some of Sarajevo's main streets.

Not long after this, Radovan became the leader of the Serb nationalists. In order to fit his new role, he deliberately held his left hand off to the side so that inquisitive onlookers could see the handle of a pistol tucked under his jacket. The transformation was fundamental. Only Radovan had no need to put a stocking over his head for his change in physiognomy to become apparent: His expression turned wild and he was no longer the person I had once known. His unassuming look evaporated, like the soul leaving the body of a dead man.

A number of writers, Radovan's contemporaries, now claim he always displayed criminal behaviour; in other words, it wasn't, as I sometimes thought, a fundamental metamorphosis. On the contrary, they were ready to testify that Karadžić frequently demonstrated his malicious nature, try as he might to cover it up. A.S. showed me scars on his forearms that served as testimony to the following incident: After realising Radovan might have reported on his private conversations (it was certainly true that the state appeared to know even the most intimate thoughts of an individual, such were the times), A.S. extinguished cigarettes on his own skin in an attempt to get Karadžić to admit to being an informer for the secret police.

Looking back on it, the belief that someone else's pain might gain the sympathy of a future war criminal seems pretty lame. But that incident, from the early '70s, demands further explanation. The generation Radovan Karadžić happened to form a part of was destined to be marked by the events of 1968. Student unrest in Sarajevo was rather mild and quite distant from the resounding volleys of global revolution, but the authorities, nevertheless, almost instantly set about to co-opt the most vocal protesters for their own purposes. They were given positions in various ministries or else simply put on the payroll of internal security services; the authorities figured their revolutionary potential would find a proper outlet in the long run. This is how the political opposition first turned into paid informers. The student demonstrations of '68 found Karadžić on the street; later, but before the war, he turned to crime. His greed truly surprised me. He even spent a year in jail, and it was indeed becoming clear that the docility he displayed in speaking to his literary contemporaries was a farce. Someone who was prepared to steal might not have far to go in order to kill. Karadžić followed through this sequence.

Those of socialism's kids who liked to dress up preferred Lenin-style hats. Karadžić's "poetic" generation was obsessed with Russian culture. One Russian trait – to take revolution as the only real event – probably had a lot to do with Radovan Karadžić's work as a war-monger. As long as there was revolutionary change: even if it came about through sheer pillage and plunder, even if it came about through absolute terror. If robbery was involved, so much the better. These were the criteria that made him the perfect errand boy for Milošević's nationalist-Stalinist project.

When I look back on the days of Karadžić's "antimilitarism", from the time he was a founder of the Greens, those plastic bags stick in my mind as one of the war's dominant objects. The refugees that this poet expelled from their homes used them – they carried only what could fit in a plastic bag. Photos and video clips from the war in Bosnia are full of those plastic bags, to the point that this harmless object turned into a precise picture of the tragedy.

I've never thought much of dwelling on someone else's deeds in retrospect. Looking at things that way says more about the person remembering than the person who actually did the deed. I rarely thought of Karadžić during the war; I was much more occupied with the problem of simply surviving. Only on days when things in Sarajevo became truly intolerable did I remember that my life had been made unbearable through Karadžić's will. There were, unfortunately, more than enough days like that, but I remember one in particular. Not because it was the most horrible, since it wasn't, but probably because it made me think of Radovan underground.

I was coming back to the city the only way you could get back to Sarajevo: through the tunnel. Water seeped in everywhere in the narrow passageway beneath the airport runway, and the mud made it even harder to get through. The tunnel was so narrow that I felt like I might collide with the oranges scattered about (they had been shuttled to the city on little wagons all that night). Since there wasn't enough air, I became so exhausted that I had to stop halfway. I didn't have the strength to take another step forward, but I had already gone too far to turn back. I was ready to just lie down and die. I found a spot that was a little wider; now I think that spot must have been made to put aside the dead so the living could pass. I stayed there for hours, underground, and thought of Radovan: We were in the Writers' Club one summer afternoon and he was telling me, with great enthusiasm, about a film he had seen the day before. The film was *Sophie's Choice*, and Radovan, speaking from the professional perspective of someone concerned with the human psyche, interpreted in great detail the various aspects of Meryl Streep's spiritual state in the scene where a German officer presents her with the following choice: which of her two children should be saved, since one would have to be killed? Underground, my hair stood on end as I remembered his rational analysis of Sophie's choice.

Radovan's psychiatric war strategy was given a truly terrifying name by the leader of his army, General Ratko Mladić: 'mind bending'. This mind bending consisted of the relentless humiliation of innocent people, and it was only in my own submission underground that I fully saw his intentions. The ghastly scene from *Sophie's Choice* was endlessly repeated in Bosnia; Karadžić's soldiers put mothers in the same position in which Meryl Streep found herself in the cinematic reconstruction of events that took place in a German concentration camp.

Karadžić must have derived at least some pleasure from the pain of his literary companion, the one who put cigarettes out on his own forearms; somewhere in his mind, he must already have conjured up some of the hellish intentions that would be realised during the war. I use the adjectival form intentionally because the reality of the war in Bosnia, as created by Radovan Karadžić for the media, has too often been called *hell* – as if our Bosnia were static, unchanging, that is, not subject to change.

At the beginning of the war, a photograph appeared in the Sarajevo daily, *Oslobodjenje*. There was a building in flames, spewing forth billows of thick, black smoke. When the photograph was taken, the smoke formed a clearly recognisable image of Radovan Karadžić. The man who put the city to flames now appeared through the smoke like a devil overseeing his destructive acts. There was no escaping it, everyone who saw the picture had precisely the same image in mind. It seems like people can only describe evil by using symbolic language. Even when the smoke over the flaming city appeared in the form of the very person who had set it on fire, that is, as a real person, it could still only be described as the devil's work. A defence mechanism: if this is the work of the devil, then it's not part of our world and evil remains distant.

The war has made me suspicious of any metaphors (and not only because poets turned into murderers). I put even less faith in metaphors derived from religious mythology: things belonging to 'that' world, a world that can only be reached by passing through death, no longer concern the living. Thus, all responsibility for the commission of evil can be abdicated. If you follow through on this metaphor – and that is why it always made me uncomfortable – then you can remove any trace of responsibility from Karadžić's acts.

This is how, to put it mildly, lies emerged victorious, and were measured out in drums of 'non-Serbian' blood. Lies were the only political means in which Radovan Karadžić had absolute faith. Since everything he did in the name of racial 'cleanliness' created a fact, so to speak – he was making a reality to fit his lies – all he had left to do was keep repeating the lies until his accumulated acts made his lies seem irrefutable. Maybe that's why it became easy for so many of our neighbours to put stockings over their heads.

For example, the claim most often repeated by Karadžić – that people of different nationalities couldn't live together in Bosnia – was simply a euphemism for racism. The truth was quite the opposite: people of different cultures had lived together for so long in Bosnia, and the ethnic mix was so deep, that any separation could only be accomplished through extreme violence and enormous bloodshed.

It was during the period when Karadžić was the most vocal champion of absolute separation along 'cultural borderlines' that I happened to thumb through the 1991-92 Sarajevo phonebook. Under the family name *Karadžić* I found 21 entries. In addition to the aforementioned poet, the rest of the entries could be fit under the following ethnic rubrics: ten Muslims, nine Serbs and one Croat. The most curious aspect of these listings was the fact that the only Croat, Mate Karadžić, carried the same first name as the leader of the Croatian nationalist party, Mate Boban. And among the Muslims, I found Ale Karadžić, Ale being a term of endearment for Alija, which is the first name of Bosnia's president, Alija Izetbegović.

On the basis of such a Bosnian ethnic inventory, any racist idea – of necessity – becomes grotesque. The most horrendous demonstration of this took place outside of Bosnia, upon the ruins of the small Croatian city of Vukovar. Vojislav Šešelj – who happens to be the only Serb with such a name, since all other Šešeljs are Croats –

celebrated his victory over the city by feasting on pork. He took the opportunity to tell news reporters that the pigs they were now eating had just fed on the remains of slaughtered Croats.

As opposed to Šešelj, Karadžić only verged on cannibalism in his pronouncements. But even though he himself never crossed the line into actual cannibalism, there was something truly barbaric in his way of thinking and his method of waging war. One of my friends, the writer A.I., used the term 'The Devils From Pale', the Serbs' HQ. The phrase never seemed precise to me. And I also thought that it embodied the typical sense of exasperation displayed by victims in the face of their persecutor, a kind of displaced awe. I think the closest anyone ever got to describing the Pale men was that boy who became so upset when I ripped his book of children's poetry. He told me a terrific story about how Chetniks multiply, like gremlins, when they come into contact with plum brandy. He managed to translate evil into a comprehensible, childish idiom. After he told me this story, I often caught him poring over maps. He was very interested in Greenland. When I asked why he wanted to go there, he replied: 'Because there's no people there.'

I myself no longer have any illusions about people. I know that someone I've just spent a nice afternoon with could knock on my door any second with a stocking on his head just the way Stojan Sljuka knocked on the door of the trolley. I haven't seen him since. As far as soccer is concerned, the epilogue to the game was gruesome: one noted professor was photographed using the decapitated head of a Muslim as a ball. So I don't have any illusions left about people or, for that matter, about nations. That's why I don't think a single nation exists that wouldn't crucify Christ. In Bosnia, it was Karadžić's Serbs who did the crucifying.

It is not only my world that has been deconstructed, but the meanings of words as well. A 'library', for example, is no longer a building filled with books but a burned-out ruin. These days, if I ever find myself in a library and wander over into the children's section, my heart freezes.

Chetniks: Serbian ultra-nationalists.

Semezdin Mehemedinović's work appears later in this anthology (pp.160-80).

MARKO VEŠOVIĆ

Translations by CHRIS AGEE / ANTONELA GLAVINIĆ

Marko Vešović was born in 1945 in Pape, Montenegro, and has lived in Sarajevo since the sixties. He studied at Sarajevo University, where he taught literature for many years. Suffused with an ironic, Rabelaisian wit, his poetry both mocks an imperfect world and celebrates the enchantments of childhood memory with gentleness and ardour. Also a highly respected critic and novelist, and an influential opponent of Serb nationalism, his essays and articles in the journal *Slobodna Bosna* (Free Bosnia) appeared to much acclaim during the siege.

Main publications: *Sunday* (1970), *Observation Post* (1976), *Sierma's Sons* (1979), *The Founder* (novel, 1982), *The Fourth Genius* (prose, 1990) and *The King and the Wreck* (1996).

Nel mezzo del cammin

You are only half-way there, and already between your hands –
Lying prostrate on the table, looking like the crayfish
You used to pull, once upon a time, from the calms in streams –
Already, the Evangelical distance grows! In those darknesses,

Sleepless and full of demons, when you wish to turn your hands
Against yourself, it so happens that some ancestor arises
From the earth and, around these wrists, claps on handcuffs!
They embrace, ever more fleetingly. They neither kindle fires

Nor quench them any longer. And with the same lassitude
They turn the key, in the morning, when among people you go forth,
And when, in the evening, you return home with the face of Buddha
Who forever banged his head – against the wall of filth!

And the touch of the fingers, through much leafing in books,
Is becoming less and less sensitive, ever more withered.
Born only yesterday, and full of century-old worries!
Last night's mushroom, it seems, remembers the Flood.

There in your lap, are they the very same
That, once upon a time for the herbarium, longed to press together
Drops of dew with a stem of dodder?
Now you don't know: what they fear, what it is that fears them.

And they have still to stroke the head of a little son
And it seems they never will. That's why they seem so weighty,
So constantly unsupple. And they watch from on
High, eagle-eyed, all there is. That's why, so easily,

They knock the ashtray off the table: they'd never shatter,
They know, a child's dream! Yet they never want
For all that much. What little they do hold
Quickly falls out of them. And each hand hovers,

Timidly, around the essence. Instead of grabbing it
By the gills, the bloody gills! Somehow they move sideways
In everything they do, like the streams' crayfish
You used to catch once, in which century was that?

Essex, on the Eve of Execution

Yes. Perhaps everything is the Lord's spittle.
Perhaps everything is a bended bow
In the hand of the blind hunter. And amen.

Yes. With the grave everything shall be washed.
What I am. And all I have done.
Everything will be wiped off like the fog from dewy grapes.

And I think it was excellent, everything that happened.
And what didn't, I think too was excellent.

But a drop of squealing light in me
Primed now with this horror, now with that,
Where will it go?

I know even lighting a pipe is an act with a hundred repercussions,
That around mountain peaks some fog must always wander.

And every blow adds a new face to me,
Out of every wound a white wood-pigeon flies.

But the Great Game in me that every
Sound of the horns startles up –
Where will it go?

Ay, with true difficulty was swallowed the multi-coloured bread
Kneaded out of heaven and earth!

But the grave's swab will cleanse everything.
No use waiting for the smoke that winds over the stake's flames
To sketch once again, as in a play, the face of the burnt.

Nor are words much use here.
They are Romans
Who eat and drink lying down.

And one giant tear will wash off everything.
What I am. And what I've never dreamt of.
Everything will be wiped off like the fog from dewy grapes.

Childhood (II)

Over the pot – tresses of steam, over the steam – Mother's face
On the face the brown bitter gloom
O the silence out of which garden apples
Stop ripening

The neighing of steeds fills the souls of virgins
With a panic like moonlight
Against the plum by the house the dragons scraped all night
The napes of their seven necks

On Sister's embroidery there's always one pattern akin
To the lay of the goldfinch
The primeval enchantment of Earth comes shielded from torment
By a million juniper-needles

Sheep's milk in a bowl gleams white to the edge of the world
The lowing of beasts leaves
The gables thicker, the sky vaster
The moonshine deeper

From a wether's liver, slaughtered for a Christening,
There arises a star in the midnight sky
Under the threshold of the house, a smell of fried meat
Tickles the nostrils of the ancestor

Some supreme tenderness radiates from the green wood
Of Mother's dowry-box
And a whole foot of waste land fits
Into the crane's cries

And again darkness slips, oily, through the eye
Of the needle in Sister's hand:
She only felt like embroidery
When wolves howled outside!

White Hawthorn in Pape

I

O, that blossoming hawthorn!
So effortlessly a king's crown
    A cloud, a god even!

It sways. And does not sway.
And always, on the eve of Whitsuntide, it traces,
    On the air, mysterious arabesques
Made of pure dream,
Gathering our looks, at least, round
    The same ancient flame.

Its scent sweetens instead of God.
It smells the way a mother's foot might
    Rock the cradle of a sick child.

II

It's been ages since it held the world in sway.
Yet the sun's eye will not burn away
    All that issues from its rare
Shadow, still older than anything.

More despised now,
    With the agitations of an exiled emperor,
Goose-pimpled in the breeze, it stands
Neither on this shore nor the other. A snake's
    Skin is sometimes to be found
On its crown. Or some unknown
Songbird carried by rapt feathers
    Beyond, or above, its flock.

Out of it, not even the devil would dare
Carve his fiddle, or a church's doorstep –
    Still less a saint, a judge, a gallows.
It secretes no healing balm.
Yet its thorn looks like a compass-needle
    Or the crabbed soul of an ancestor.

III

That one-storey tree.
Its sweep is not skywards, but downwards:
    It wants, first, to sink its fairy-roots deeper
Than the pickaxe can reach;
To breach the barren soil, and lean the soul
    Against its soured secrets.
It's not a thirst shooting up,
But a growth towards the dead, spread sideways. And closer and closer
    To our own house door.

It's not history.
Not even the real. Yet what boils in it
    Will never be driven out
By this flame, that bill-hook.
For isn't its every needle a guardian
    Of empyrean pledges?

IV

Isn't the hawthorn an hour of honey
That will not let the chaos in?
   A gemcutter that polishes precious stones
In the eye of the whirlwind of black powers?

Standing there like a messenger
   With a telegram bearing serious news –
For a whole lifetime, have I simply watched
With half-lidded pupils, threading on a black string
   The white pearl?

V

For our time and its
Do not cross; it is less
   Thisworldly after each blossoming.

Under the hawthorn's bark
The seraph is still asleep that after every flight
   Is closer to eternal youth
And the ever-burgeoning mystery.
O, that swan amongst trees
   Takes no notice of us.

But, at least, a grain of blueness that keeps watch
In every thorn banishes
   The ghosts of the midnight pillow

And washes the dross of evil off
Our words, bowls and blood;
   And everything under the sky, as on an anvil,
Becomes simple, and clean...

Grave/Cave

You, Arab script
You abound in sabres
And new Moons!

In the Ropushnjak cave
The dragons have vanished
But gone too is the treasure they slept on.

On this road, God knows when,
Barbarians cantered by on horses –

Look anywhere, and we're still choking
From the dust raised
By their hooves.

And the bat-like, hundred-eared
Child's soul is gone
That once heard the drift of padding
Snowflakes.

Are your petals, *world*, falling from this orange blossom?
Or is it just more and more shallow in me,
More and more illegible

Just as each day
These sabres, these new Moons
Are becoming less and less clear

On the crooked turban-stone?

Summa Summarum

The leaves of the ilex by the graveyard
Whisper prophetically.

And barley-corn ripens
Like those actors who
In the same role for a hundredth time
Stand forth before the audience.

Yet do not extol,
To the skies, your native land.
It ought to extol you.

Seen from this cloud
These meadows and fields
Are a stamp album;

And to the ant a smoke ring
Twirling from your cigarette
Is a whole new landscape!

And stop threatening for once
To return next time
To this handful of land without history
Only in the shape of a rider in bronze.

And before you leave
Stroke the bark of these trees
Which all the while have given you
Free lessons in standing tall!

ILIJA LADIN

Translations by KEN SMITH / IGOR KLIKOVAC

Ilija Ladin (a *nom de plume* for Ilija Kozić) was born in 1929 in Stratinska, near Banja Luka, and studied French literature at Sarajevo. Intensely devoted to his *métier* – there are several versions of almost all his poems – he is a poet of wit, heresy and religious insight, whose frequent use of repetition can often have the quality of a mantra. He taught secondary school for many years and is currently a freelance writer. A member of the 'gusle'* or sixties generation of poets, he was highly influential among the 'rock' generation of poets that emerged in the early eighties.

Main publications: *Nothing Before You* (1968), *From Sky to Here* (1973), *Poems on a Cabin* (1975), *Bird Songs* (1979), *The Suffering Has Begun* (1986), *That's How I Am Tonight* (1989), *To the Muses I Apologise* (1990), and *Mister Mo* (1995).

Like Krle when he smokes marijuana

Really God
How many times
The world has turned
foul

And you again
Labour?
Struggle?

Like Krle when he smokes marijuana
– What? he says Once? Take another puff
She says nothing to you
The first time

Like Krle
When he smokes
Marijuana

There's two already
I
Don't understand

---

* *gusle*: a one-stringed folk fiddle popular in the Balkans.

Running

Under that sack that is called life
Running running
And not looking back
Yet
And with the ninety-nine names you carry in your heart
And with the Ark of the Covenant with God
Which you carry also
Running running

No not yet:
Do not look back yet
Lot's wife
Is a bad example

Mustapha's bags

Packed bags
For a movement and a trip
Are in the hall Soon
Empty houses
Full of ghosts

Will be for the persecutors
Only the day
Is waiting

Sorrow for the homeland
Kids will
Forget Only the old
Will slowly die from it

With it
The great writers
Will live

Only the day
Is waiting
To see what happens to the persecuted

A slug's nightmare

Thus being brought to life he was naked
a bare naked slug
Then he hid himself in his shell
But again naked he was
a bare naked slug
Then he hid himself in the weeds
But again naked he was
a bare naked slug
Then he hid himself in a crack in the Earth
But again naked he was
a bare naked slug
Then he hid himself in its heart
into the Earth's heart
But again naked he was
a bare naked slug
And they already after him
set out for him
slugokill
to get rid
of him

And everything was licked up
but for his coarse
tongue!
A trace of his oh what a splendour!

My death in the trenches

Throw this body out of the trench!
Take his weapons
Take the clothes off him

And peel off the skin listen
He's one of ours!

So the other side don't make shoeleather of him

He's one of ours cut off his head too!

So they can't make a scarecrow
Listen

He's one of ours

And suck out the eyes

And our vision of the world
take

take it with you
away from them

While you still can…

He's one of ours

A stone wedding

I was heading home
a lyre in my hand
followed by a crowd of girls
screaming all exalted
I was heading home
a sword in my hand
beheading every dragon
that came my way
For the King's daughter
I was heading home
a sceptre in my hand
on a golden carriage through triumphal arches
But I didn't bring
The bride
You honourable old men of the tribe!

A lightning has burned
all those praying
in the hovel

raising high their hands
the eyelids
and the heart

They survived the hell –
who held each others' hands
man beside man:

that was kolo naokolo*
and the singing in kolo
instead of praying

And they spread
that electricity
touching the ground together with the dancing feet:
                                        and saved themselves!

Honourable old men of the tribe!
Saved themselves:
those who were in the kolo!

*lit. 'round and around'

From sky to here

From the sky to here
the way is much shorter

From sky to here
birds don't need wings
nor have flowers ever needed
a scent

Peak of the roof

A man climbs onto the house
a builder

He's merry
he yells
clamours
shouts

He built the scaffolding he's standing on
God didn't want it higher
a soil he touches first when he makes a stand
thrown out of the mother's womb
that's somewhat higher

Women almost touched him:
they give him gifts

Now he praises their hands
above his
builder's

because he sticks everything on a stick
he raises it high
to flutter in the wind

Soon he will come down from up there
all broken and alone

And only the chimneysweeps will sometimes climb up on the roof
Black as night
Dumb as the ground

I was air

I was air
and in the storm a voice
and you didn't hear me

I was water
and in the flood a voice
and you didn't hear me

I was fire

and in the flames a voice
But even your own
ashes

told you
nothing
Puff!

FERIDA DURAKOVIĆ

Translations into English and Irish by NUALA NÍ DHOMHNAILL/
ANTONELA GLAVINIĆ

Ferida Duraković was born in 1957 in Olovo, near Sarajevo, and studied Yugoslav literatures at Sarajevo University. Before the war she was the Director of the Youth Cultural Centre in Sarajevo and also managed a popular bookshop burnt down during the siege. A poet of profound feeling, her clear and sensuous language mixes a sensitivity to the emotional effects of syntax with a miniaturist's focus. She continues to live in Sarajevo and now works for the P.E.N. Centre of Bosnia-Herzegovina.

Main publications: *A Masked Ball* (1977), *Eyes That Watch Me* (1982), *A Little Night Music* (1989), and *Heart of Darkness* (1994).

From the Textbook of Slavic Mythology

When the conquerors, monotheistic and unimaginative
tore down and burnt Perun
made of Slavic lime
to prove there is no god in wood

they hadn't the foggiest clue, stupid clods that they were,
that only God can grant this gift to them,
that the only fire that can both warm and feed them
is divine fire.

In every tree lives thunder
and in every thunder Perun
who consumes himself in fire
and in every Perun, look, there is a Slav
lamenting loudly this world's woes deep under a lime tree.

On What I Have Known for a Long Time

The bells sound and resound.
At the door of the house the years
stand and patiently wait
for the rooms to be emptied,
for the floors to wear out and the fire
to go out and the cockerel clocks to stop.

Lulled to sleep
on my mother's shoulders to the smell of vanilla,
the piteous angels forget their terrible task.

On the shelves there is always a supper waiting,
in her hands there is always some warmth.

Sometimes, after the wars,
I am back here to stay
and I know:

every single day,
every single moment,
in this home is waiting
a tall, blue vase.

Good Evening, the Guest Is Gone

One, two, three walnuts on the table –
those hidden essences you can only attain
by destroying a world, and a single lone bowl
empty of fruit, without oranges or apples –
people have eaten their beautiful bodies
and thrown their outward appearance in plastic bags onto the rubbish
        dump.

Three walnuts, therefore, and a bowl and the guest
who is gone, whose basic absence
fills the hollow in the chair as if it were a soul.

It is time to get up and to open the window and let fresh air and
    darkness in.

Three walnuts, therefore, and the bowl, and the guest
who is gone, and a basic inertia which does not allow
any change in this general picture
that devastates and amazes in its sheer simplicity.

Three walnuts, therefore, and the bowl, and the guest
who is gone, and inertia
and a dark eye, peering through the windowpane, into whose pupil
    this image sinks.

November, Raging Through Rooms

Alone: at last. Herself and the darkness in the essence of things.
Little black men are knocking and clicking their tongues in old
    cupboards.
While the dark is at work, she wants *to sleep. Perchance to dream.*
Not so fast. Get up, sister, get up and write letters. The dark
is nothing so much as the absence of light. Let
the dark work for us.
It will tire itself out before dawn. Here I am over, beyond,
sinking into myself as if into a chair, and it is not difficult
they taught me: to plough
                to dig
                deep through myself, by myself,
and not to try to work miracles with a single look.
Objects advise me of what is happening to my loved ones:
a chair moving in the dark – means one of us is gone;
a book falling off a shelf – means they are raging through rooms;
a creak in the floor – means the over-aged lads are skiving off for a walk.
Making lists and counting them is how I collect my thoughts;
            You'd better do so too.
On the left beyond your hearing there is a switch;
sister, sister, let's call it light.

It's April

and life so unattractive; the dead earth suddenly turns vampire
and breathes, breathes, breathes, with it begin to breathe
the souls of the dead, in harmony,
following orders from *the cruellest month*;
they yearn to lie down quietly among sweet flowers.

The mirrors in the room get fidgetty
looking into the terror-filled eyes of old men
and in the dumb fear of old men they arouse the desire
to breathe, breathe, breathe……

The whole sky could fit
into a dirty puddle of rain.

Georg Trakl on the Battlefield Revisited, 1993

On high, above the planes, dwells God , the beloved,
eyes gleaming gold above the Sarajevo gloom.
Fruit-blossom and mortarshells both fall beyond my window.
Madness and me. Alone. We are alone. So alone.

Athcuairt ar Georg Trakl ar Pháirc an Áir, 1993

Ins na hardaibh, os cionn na n-eitléan, tá cónaí ar Dhia,
a shúile órga ag glioscarnach i ndoircheacht Sarajevo.
Titeann bláthanna crann is diúracáin lasmuigh dem fhuinneoga.
An buile is mé fhéin in aontíos. Inár n-aonar. Inár n-aonaráin,

The Writer Contemplates His Homeland While a Famous Postmodernist Enters the City

For a long time everything has repeated itself most cruelly
and yet everything is happening for the first time:
the face of a young man whose life all night
has been draining out through your hands, from the hole
in his back. The face of the soldier
by the bus station, with the pleasant May sky
frozen permanently in his open eyes – *you are making it up.*
I declare – this is not the calm and distant face of History
And a little pool of blood; in its middle a hunk of bread
soaked in blood like that now fabled morning *Bregov milk* –
you're making it up, I repeat, for the very first time:
the Sarajevan clay that falls on the big feet of the boy
in his Reebok trainers as they dangle
from a makeshift bier made from a cupboard door. No, you
are not to be trusted, you have entered the heart
of darkness that erupted and gushed forth into daylight.
You are an unreliable witness, and biased at that. That's why
the Professor has arrived, entirely Parisian in mien, *Mes enfants*
he started, and his fingers repeat it for him: *Mes
enfants, mes enfants, mes enfants*, in the middle
of the Academy of Science the old greybeards could think
only of his shirt, glaringly and conspicuously white.
Mes enfants, this is the death of Europe. Then he changes
it all into a film, into frames, into mouthfuls like
histoire, Europe, like *responsabilité* and, of course
les Bosniacs. Look here, that's the right way to look History
in the face, not like you: in the crude irresponsible fragments,
the sniper shot that penetrates deep into the skull,
the graves already covered over by irredeemable grass,
your hands placed across the image of
Edvard Munch, who himself, once upon a time,
also made everything up, with no hope.

REZAK HUKANOVIĆ

FROM The Tenth Circle of Hell: A Memoir of Life in the Death Camps of Bosnia (1996)

Translated by AMMIEL ALCALAY

Although written in the third person, *The Tenth Circle of Hell* is a first-hand account of life in a Serb concentration camp. Rezak Hukanović was seized on 30 May 1992 in his home town of Prijedor, a small north-western Bosnian city of 112,000, where he worked as a journalist. The course of aggression against non-Serbs in Prijedor was typical of the war in Bosnia: the occupying Serb nationalist forces systematically seized and, very often, murdered the local élites – mayors, doctors, lawyers, judges, teachers, engineers and cultural figures. Hukanović has explained that he chose to use the third person because he felt, at the time, that the brutal events he endured – as well as the complicit behaviour of friends and neighbours – must have been happening to someone else.

Later that afternoon the prisoners were loaded onto a bus, from which waved a big Serbian flag mounted on one of the side mirrors. Three soldiers sat in the front seats facing them. The bus started moving. It went straight to the underpass, then right, then left toward the cellulose and paper factory, before turning down the street running along the banks of the Sana River. Djemo looked at the Old City. Tongues of flame rose high above the burning roofs. Dense whirls of smoke gathered into huge black clouds. The Old City, that island in the river surrounded by the Sana and the Berek, looked like an enormous torch. 'That's how all your houses will burn,' said one of the soldiers.

Djemo just kept quiet, impotently gritting his teeth and sighing in despair, feeling almost unbearably humiliated. It seemed to him that he would remember this image of the Old City in flames until his dying day. That part of the city was the source of many sweet memories. He fell in love for the first time right there, on the banks of the Berek, and it was there that he smoked his first cigarette. The dances held on the stage of the open-air theatre were unforgettable, not only for the people of Prijedor but for those from other places who came to spend the summer. And swimming at night in the Sana… memories kept reeling as his throat tightened. And the misery flowed from his eyes. His body felt weighed down by helplessness and humiliation. He reached toward his pocket for a cigarette but remembered that his cigarettes had been taken away at the police station.

Their heads bent down, their eyes bereft of hope, the prisoners lurched forward as the bus led them into the unknown. The Serb soldiers in the front of the bus occasionally greeted passers-by with three raised fingers in the traditional Serb salute; they also sang some strange, unintelligible songs. One group of villagers in fatigues and muddy boots signalled to the bus driver to stop. They asked the escorting soldiers to hand over the prisoners. Looking over the frightened men on the bus, one villager said, 'Those are *Ustasha*' – the Croatian fascists who collaborated with Hitler in World War II. 'They should all be taken care of using the "shortcut",' he said, holding his hand like a knife across his neck, his face twisting in an eerie grimace of hate. He and his friends were ready to lynch the prisoners on the spot, though they didn't know any of them.

One of the soldiers mumbled something and ordered the driver to shut the door and drive on. Through the window Djemo could see the wide expanse of the plain at the foot of the Kozara Mountains, just where the turf of tilled soil reached its highest elevation. Fertile, ploughed land, sown with wheat, extending as far as the eye could see. 'Who will harvest it?' wondered Djemo. Abandoned cattle, cows, horses, sheep, and newborn lambs grazed in the fields. They wandered around scorched houses as long spits of flame and pillars of smoke soared high above them. In front of the houses, fresh linen still hung on lines stretched across the courtyards. No one had expected such evil.

Djemo remembered the words of the great novelist Ivo Andrić: 'Only in the Balkans can anything happen anytime.' And it had happened, the worst that can happen, right here by the mountain range, where history marches in military step. In the Kozara Mountains people had always started again from scratch, after every battle, after every plague. The mountain people were tough, but it was also true that no one could love their patch of sky, their fields and houses and mountains, as much as they did.

In earlier wars the locals had fought to defend Bosnia's border region from various enemies, but now… what exactly was happening now? Who were these mighty warriors who fled their farms, leaving behind half-empty beer bottles, to take up cannons and machine guns, to fire mortars and bullets, heedless of what they aimed at or how many rounds they shot? Once, not so long ago, people had made sacrifices; they had gone without food for the greater good. Now they were defying the legal authorities to arm what had once been everyone's army, the Yugoslav People's Army, taking refuge in the five-pointed star and the attribute 'People's'. And now that army was pounding Bosnians with the very same weapons they had acquired to defend themselves from any possible enemy – only the enemy, it turned out, had been living right next door, right down the street. Until just yesterday Bosnians had shared everything, drinking coffee together, going to parties and funerals together, visiting each other, marrying each other, but now…

To the old song's words 'Where the People's Army marches…',

Djemo would have added '...is a land where grass no longer grows'. These were strange times. Bosnia trembled as if it had been hit by a powerful earthquake. But an earthquake comes and goes. This upheaval just kept on coming. Was this bus trip the beginning of something still worse? The people beaten up – what were they guilty of? And what about the others, staring at the floor of the bus, their eyes filled with fear? The new Serbian authorities had nothing to blame them for, other than that their very existence was a reminder that Bosnia had long been home to Muslims and Croats as well as Serbs. Now Serbs were destroying mosques and churches and even digging up graveyards. Such crimes were well organised and harked back to times everyone thought had been forgotten. Irrational hatred flowed from the darkest parts of their souls and stared out from their bloodshot eyes. The reaction of most people was silence, fearful silence.

The bus stopped outside the administration building of the iron ore mine at Omarska, only a few miles from the village of the same name. On one side, looted cattle grazed in the mowed fields, while across from them the mining embankments – busy with workers until only days before – lay remote and isolated, seared by the unbearable heat. Two huge buildings stood in the centre, separated by a wide asphalt lot with two smaller buildings. The prisoners were ordered to get off the bus with their arms raised over their heads, holding up three fingers on each hand. Two rows of fully armed soldiers opened a path through which they had to walk. Five men were pulled out of the line; the others were taken into one of the big buildings. Among the five selected, Djemo recognised Tewfik, a local actor whom everyone called 'Cheapskate'. Within minutes a burst of machine-gun fire rang out. Cheapskate would never 'break a leg' on stage again...

With every arriving busload, the room got more and more crowded. Djemo's son Ari arrived, along with his cousins Fadil, Mirsad, and Fudo, and Fudo's son Elijan. By Djemo's count, over twenty buses arrived before dark.

The pattern repeated itself the next day. Over the course of two days more than three thousand inhabitants of Prijedor and its outlying villages were arrested in their homes in these inconceivable raids and brought to the Serb prison at Omarska. Among the prisoners, whose only fault was being Muslim or Croat, were intellectuals, teachers, engineers, police officers, craftsmen. Djemo recognised the mayor of Prijedor, the Honourable Mr Muhamed Čehajić. How absurd such a title seemed now.

The prisoners were given nothing to eat for the first four days. They slept on a tiled floor. Djemo found a cardboard box, broke it up, and put it on the floor for himself and his son to use as a bed. The stale air was hard to breathe and dried out their throats. On the fifth day they were ordered to line up for food. Their hunger was unbearable. Everyone swarmed to the door, and they were taken away in groups of thirty. Ari was in the third group; Djemo was way back in the tenth. When Djemo's group came up, they were told there was no more food. They went back to their places, writhing in pain. Later all prisoners would be given food once a day: a couple of cabbage leaves with a few beans, covered in tepid water, and a piece of bread that seemed to be made of soapsuds. They would be allowed only two minutes to eat.

Most of the time the prisoners were beaten on the way to and from the canteen where they ate. That route wound through a narrow corridor that branched off at the end and led to a staircase on the right. Upstairs, prisoners were interrogated. Back downstairs, on the left, was the canteen. The guards would pour water on a worn-out patch of glazed cement to make the corridor more slippery. If a prisoner fell, the guards would pounce on him like famished beasts at the sight of a carcass. Using whips made of thick electrical cable, they beat the fallen prisoner all the way up the stairs for the inevitable interrogation – or simply to finish the job they had already started […]

The prisoners took care of their bodily needs using a plastic bucket by the tin door of the garage. When somebody took a leak, the others gathered around to cup their hands and catch the urine, wetting their chapped lips with it and even drinking it. They slept standing up, because there was no space to lie down. Those next to the wall raised their hands high above their heads, keeping them against the wall; paint ran under their palms from the heat and moisture, trickling down their arms to create hideous reliefs.

Once, for no reason at all, a drunken guard let go a burst of machine-gun fire at the garage door. Djemo and his fellow prisoners could hear screams and cries for help. Word spread that one prisoner in the garage had been killed and four seriously wounded. The four were taken somewhere, supposedly to a hospital, but nobody saw them again.

One time Djemo caught sight of the miserable prisoners in the garage through the wide door to his area. A group of about ten of them were chosen and taken out some forty yards in front of the garage. They were ordered to undress completely. The prisoners began taking off their worn, ragged clothes and putting them in a pile as four guards looked on. The guards were completely drunk, as anyone could tell by the way they moved. As the prisoners stripped, bashfully using their hands to try to cover their nakedness, the guards fixed their cynical glares upon them even more intently. One big man, over six feet tall, refused to strip. His beard was long, a sign that he had been imprisoned for quite some time. He simply kept quiet and didn't move. He stood with his head bowed, mutely watching. One of the guards came up to him, put the barrel of his rifle to the man's neck, and said something to him. The man just stood there, without moving a single part of his body. 'The poor guy's going to get it, they'll kill him,' said someone behind Djemo. Djemo didn't turn around or respond but kept looking through the upper part of the glass door that separated the inmates from the guards. He was watching to see what would happen to this defiant figure and the other men from Kozarac.

The guard, seeing that the man was steadfast in his intention not to carry out the order, aimed his rifle upward and fired several shots into the air. Except for some quail in a nearby tree flying away out of sight, nothing happened. The man stood stubbornly in place without making the slightest movement. While bluish smoke still rose from the rifle barrel, the guard struck the clothed man in the middle of the head with the rifle butt, once and then again, until the man fell. Then the guard handed his rifle to another guard and moved his hand to his belt. A knife flashed in his hand, a long army knife.

He bent down, grabbing hold of the poor guy's hair with his free hand. Another guard joined in, continuously cursing. He, too, had a flashing knife in his hand. The two other guards backed off a little and trained their rifles on the nine naked prisoners, observing their every move. The guards with the knives started using them to tear away the man's clothes. After only a few seconds, they stood up, their own clothes covered with blood. The air resounded with a long, loud, and painful wail. It sent shivers through all who heard it.

Never in all his life was Djemo to see a more horrifying sight. The poor man stood up a little, or rather tried to stand up, still letting out excruciating screams. He was covered with blood. One guard took a water hose from a nearby hydrant and directed the strong jet at the poor prisoner. A mixture of blood and water flowed down his exhausted, gaunt, naked body as he bent down repeatedly, like a wounded Cyclops, raising his arms above his head, then lowering them toward the jet of water to fend it off; his cries were those of someone driven to insanity by pain. And then Djemo, and everyone else, saw clearly what had happened: the guards had cut off the man's sexual organ and half of his behind.

After that Djemo couldn't remember anything. The shocking sight of that horror momentarily numbed his mind. Only later was he told that the poor man, after succumbing to the torture, was taken to a garbage container, doused with gasoline, and burned. The other men were taken back to the garage. When the interrogations began, the garage gradually started to empty. Eventually no more than fifty people were left, living witnesses to incarceration in the infamous garage. A constant fear permeated the prisoners' very bones, spreading throughout their bodies. It took great stoicism to endure the contempt and torture. Days went by, one day like the one before, and each day even more like the one that followed. Hot, humid days followed by rain, then more rain followed by heat and humidity. Frail bodies became even frailer. The pale faces bore expressions of immeasurable suffering, irretrievable loss of peace of mind, and human dignity devastated beyond repair. Movement around the already tight space was reduced to a minimum in order to save energy. Lined up along the walls on their cardboard beds in their ragged sweaters and jackets, the men, looking as if they had been cemented into the darkness, talked less and less. They believed that they were saving their energy, forgetting for the time the offenses fate had inflicted on them. They knew that they had to get to the other side of the abyss [...]

Most of the victims who came through Omarska were from Kozarac; their homes had also been hit the hardest. The residents of Kozarac were either killed on the spot or driven out in the long columns of pain flowing from the points of the daggers held by former neighbours. They were marched into the camps around Prijedor: Brezičani, Keraterm, Trnopolje, Omarska. Among the two thousand people from Kozara crammed into Omarska were Kasim Grozdanić, a fifty-five-year-old shopkeeper, and his son Suad, nicknamed 'Sudo' by his friends. They spent their days as prisoners in the hangar, the building across the runway from Djemo's dorm. They were captured when they and some of their neighbours had attempted, through the hail of artillery shells that destroyed their village, to get to Mount Kozara and then across the mountains, under the protection of the forest. Wanting only to get as far as possible from the hell that had enveloped them, they didn't even know where they were heading. They were captured along with hundreds of others and taken to the police station in Prijedor. After being tortured for two days, they were transferred to Omarska. Kasim's brother and his three sons were with them.

First they were placed in 'Twenty-Six', the notorious dorm above the hangar, and then down below in the hangar's huge hall where more than a thousand prisoners spent their days. The bare cement, covered with puddles of gasoline and dirty motor oil, was all they had to sleep on. The space they slept in was surrounded by a ring of barbed wire. There were smaller dorms upstairs, where between forty-five and fifty prisoners were kept. In the highest part of the hangar, about forty-five feet above the floor, pigeons nestled in between the asbestos room and the huge steel girders. At every flap of their wings, lice plummeted off their feathers onto the poor wretches below. The unbearable stench made everyone nauseous. There were no windows that opened anywhere, only tiny glass brick skylights at the peak of the roof. Occasionally the guards opened the big doors through which broken equipment had been ferried in and out in the old days.

Kasim and Sudo were right by the steps in the hangar that led to the small dorms, the former offices of the mine administrators. Kasim had taken off his old windbreaker and put it down for his son to lie on. Sudo just lay on the bare and dirty cement. Anxiety was deeply etched into Kasim's sunken cheeks. White shocks, premature signs of old age, ran through his hair. His face had a yellowish pallor, but his eyes still expressed an odd sense of defiance.

Sudo was just twenty-four. The spark of manhood was in his eyes, since he had left youth behind. Tall and well built, he had been the kind of guy any girl would fall head over heels for, but he was fading away now, from day to day. His youthful face had taken on a stony colour as his eyes began to sink and lose their shine, the dark circles growing beneath them. His skin had begun to sag and wrinkle. His skinny legs stuck out, as if planted in the cement. Like so many others, he had contracted dysentery from the bad food and filthy conditions. Could there be any misery worse than this, rushing for the toilet every second, as your bleeding guts try to force themselves out? Often such a prisoner couldn't make it and lost control, the excrement running down the legs of his pants as it soiled the bodies huddled along the floor on the way to the toilet. There was always a guard in the hangar next to the toilet, ready to administer a beating.

Sudo got so weak he couldn't even go and eat. So his father didn't go either. Kasim didn't want to leave his son alone for even a minute. With some German marks he had managed to hide, Kasim bought some biscuits to feed Sudo. 'You have to eat, son, it'll make you feel better. You have to get better,' Kasim would say, as if he were uttering some magical incantation. Sudo would prop himself up, leaning on one arm, just enough to let his father put the biscuit in his mouth. Then he'd chew for a long time until, a painful grimace on his face, he forced it down, choking on a coughing fit brought on by his stomach cramps.

The overwhelming heat pinched at Kasim's eyes, and he often felt the need to cry, to just scream out loud with all his strength. It seemed to him that doing so would have made things easier, but he didn't do it, because of his son. His misery was gathered into the few glistening drops that slid slowly down his parched cheeks. But his eyes retained the fury of curses as he cracked his knuckles and raised his head upward, toward the sky, to pray to God.

'Out, everybody out,' barked one of the guards as he came in and stood with his back to the huge doors. Kasim knew that Sudo would have to go out too; he didn't dare ask whether his son could stay. And even if the guard had said he could, there was no way Kasim could trust him. Kasim helped his son up onto his weak legs and managed to get him outside in front of the hangar.

'Take off all your clothes, everything,' one of the guards shouted angrily. 'We can't even go into the hangar because of your stink.' Another guard held a thick rubber hose that blasted a stream of water onto the asphalt surface. Kasim felt unspeakable shame that his son had to see and endure such humiliation. The skinny bodies looked even more pathetic without the rags covering them. They were taken out ten at a time to be hosed down. Kasim and Sudo's turn came. When they were just a few yards from the guard with the hose, he began to douse them. The powerful stream of cold water beat down on them like truncheons. Laughing and joking, the guards kept up the merciless game between the water and the paltry, weakened bodies for a long time.

Sudo twisted, turning his back to the water. Biting his lower lip from pain, he tried to protect himself with his hands as he avoided looking at his father. Kasim tried to use his own body to shield his son from the powerful impact of the water. Some men screamed as the water pounded on their open wounds. The healthier ones tried to catch a few drops of water in their mouths to moisten their parched throats, but the pressure of the water almost choked them. The guards just kept pointing at them and laughing cynically. They thoroughly enjoyed the spectacle of helplessness. Even though it didn't last long, it seemed to go on forever. Afterward the prisoners pulled on the tattered remains of their clothes and ran back to their spots in the hangar. Kasim and Sudo were among the last to return.

As they entered the hangar, the guards clubbed them on their backs and heads with truncheons, cursing all the while. Kasim's shirt got caught on the door handle. Before he knew it, at least ten truncheons were pummelling his back. He tugged at the shirt until it tore, freeing him to run into the fenced-off area in the hangar and escape an even fiercer beating.

That night Sudo ran a fever and the pains in his stomach got worse.

An awful and treacherous boom rang through his head. He barely recognised the voices of the men around him. Dimly, he saw his father's anxious face and felt Kasim's fingers stroking his hair, soaked in sweat. The light in the bulb shining through the broken fixture outside created patterns across his face. 'Dad, I...,' Sudo whispered, barely audible, as his father inched closer to hear what his son was saying. 'I don't regret dying, Dad, as long as I can stop looking at this. What did we ever do to them anyway?' Kasim looked away so that his son wouldn't see the tears in his eyes.

From the tiny skylights above, the first light of day began to appear. Sudo's breathing became more difficult, then softer and shorter. Life slowly ebbed from his withered body. Little by little, the light of his twenty-four years extinguished itself. 'Please, Dad...' and his last words withered on his lips. A heavy, dead silence reigned throughout the hangar. Off in a corner, someone cursed God.

Kasim got up, straightened himself, and stood still for a long time, as if he had turned to stone. His tears dried. His face twisted, contorted by the hatred rising within him. He bit his fist to staunch the sobbing that, like a flood, felt as if it would drown him. He looked but could see and hear nothing. He didn't weep with his eyes but with his soul, with a father's pain. With the death of his son, lying here beside him, he had lost his main reason for living. The image of his dead son burned itself into his heart and would smoulder there, like a glowing ember. How would he tell his wife, if she was still alive, that their son – her darling boy, the apple of her eye – was gone? And what about Suada, Sudo's dear sister?

Kasim just stood there as a guard came up to him. 'What's the matter with this one over here?' he asked, kicking the lifeless body. Kasim didn't say a word, but his eyes passed over the guard like a dagger. His look, full of hatred and contempt, was almost like a stab in the face. 'This one's been dead at least three days by now. Get this garbage out of here,' the guard said, not bothering to hide his barbaric cruelty. Kasim's mouth began to move, to say something or spit in the guard's face, but his numbed lips couldn't budge. He stood there like a deaf mute, looking at Sudo's dead body as if he were pledging an oath to some invisible form of justice that he would one day fulfil in his son's name.

Kasim kept standing like that when his brother and his brother's sons carried the dead body out and took it over by the White House. They left Sudo's body on the grass where a few other corpses were piled. Later all the corpses were loaded onto the yellow truck. 'His youth will be buried somewhere in these trenches,' Kasim said quietly. 'Will I ever find out where?' He would live the rest of his life settling accounts.

RANKO SLADOJEVIĆ

Translations by HARRY CLIFTON / ANTONELA GLAVINIĆ

Ranko Sladojević was born in 1951 in Fojnica, near Sarajevo, and studied German language and literature at Sarajevo University, receiving his doctorate in 1988. He taught in the German Department until the outbreak of the war, edited the important literary journals *Život (Life)* and *Lica (Faces)*, and worked for Radio Sarajevo. Influenced by the 'new sensibility' of German writing in the sixties and early seventies, his early work was distinguished by formal experimentation and the exploration of colloquial speech, though his war poems mark a return to traditional forms. He is also a distinguished critic of contemporary literature in the former Yugoslavia and Germany, and has translated poetry and philosophy from the German. He now lives in Heidelberg.

Main publications: *Conversations* (1973), *Summer Dream* (1989), *Late Night Show* (1990), and *Feeding the Eagle* (1991, a novel).

Summer Holidays in Hell

Yes, that's us. You've got our whereabouts right.
Through which agency did you go?
There are more beautiful places. Even so,
What's done is done. All praise to the Almighty!

Now for the house rules. Citizens of hell
Live on detonations, water and bread.
It's a good life. What with the brickless walls,
The glassless windows, you can take it as read

We love freedom, yes, and we love change.
All this had been whole till yesterday
Then tedium set in. We took the plunge –

An instant, an eruption, cleared the air.
But settle down, and titivate your body.
You are to pass your summer holidays here.

Death-Bed

Sunday – a pause in time. When everything
Halts, except for the tinkle of spoons
On pale porcelain. Sunday lunch – it sticks in the craw.
An emptied day, without morning –
One long afternoon instead. A cruel
Rest-day, abandonment in which the voices
Of sports commentators chatter – *Gooal!*
In Tuzla the home side leads 3-0. Switch channels
To half-time in Split. Oh dear, dear God,
The cities, names. The world – it still existed then,
Fused in one enthusiasm...
                              Burnt-out
Sundays without football now, the summers empty,
Winters solitary. In the twilight you come
And rest your lips, smooth as cherries,
Ice-cold, on my cheek. In the twilight you leave
And Sunday dies. Before sleep
The news and politics, sports results –
Proof that the day existed.
Sunday – I close my eyes,
And lonely without me, it dies.

The Angel of Winter

Next to the room I sleep in, real, pale winter prevails. Enough to open
the balcony door to see it for myself. Thick grains of snow gleam
in the hanging gardens. My white footprints are the only sign that
someone lives in the room. On the other side, another balcony –
naked frozen concrete greets me there. For snow falls in different
directions. Sometimes it covers the south balcony, sometimes the
north. The first snow I diligently picked up and stuffed in plastic
bags, so as not to shower my unknown neighbours below. Needless
worry, needless job. No one else touches their snow, everyone lets
it drift off the balcony of its own accord. The new snow I left as it
was, fallen quite close to my bed. I hardly noticed it. For twenty

days I had lain in a death-like sleep. I curled on the floor, desireless, flummoxed by love. All my clocks still with me – cuckoo, wall and digital, whirring on the cupboards, and the frightened heartbeats of alarm clocks, quartz and manual, amplified voices. Dawnings, darkenings in the room were my only divisions of time. I didn't touch them for days. Then I wound them up and they woke me. They blazed away like fire in a hearth, warming my weak breath, bringing a glow to my cheeks. I gathered the dust off everything, swept it out from under the sleeping objects – a weak, forgotten sheen came through it all. When night came, I crept into bed, discovering again the pleasure of sleep. All at once, the room went quiet. The clocks, too, went quiet, and my sleep, as if linked to their ticking, dispersed. In that silence, I was unfrightened by the soft, persistent knocking at balcony doors. It was coming from outside. I listened with eyelids shut tight and didn't answer. A moment later, a steady quiet breath blew over my head. My eyelids no longer a sanctuary, I opened them wide. Milky luxurious light pervaded the room – through its rays shone thousands of snowflakes. It snowed everywhere – on the tops of cupboards, in the corners of the room. The balcony doors, the glass on the windows vanished. I was snowed-in, snowed-out, but still under wraps. My guest had knocked, though he could have come in unannounced to take his shelter. I hoped he would get his bearings. I had no wish to disturb him in his newfound sanctuary, in the room which he transfigured. I went back to sleep, and found in the morning little footprints, and around them two shallow, barely visible impressions – where the wings had been. My guest had absented himself again. I wound the clocks once more, and a new night drew peacefully on.

The Pillow

Why is this pillow black,
The little boy wonders, lying back.
Inside him, a bullet. How did it enter?
Through the window, crazy splinter!

And the window itself, how black it is!
Nothing can be seen outside
Or in the room. Behind his eyes
It's blackout, Lights Out, time has died.

Call that a game? To get up, go out,
For the bombs to stop, for the silly war
Not to be such a bore...

Is there anything sweet?
Only some sugar. He'd kill for an ice-cream!
Only the voice-overs, and the screams.

Lunch on Day Seventy-Seven

A typical conversation with the neighbours –
What will be the outcome of all this?
Hopefully, solutions will be found,
The quicker the better. Really, as it is,

Excitement's killing everyone. Who knows
When next we see our missing sons and daughters
Whether they'll be recognisable?
Danger around us, like a gambler's throw,

But it has been asked of us to linger here
Eating winter lunch off summer plates.
Still, the Great One gives us our desserts –

If only He would let the suffering stop! –
And coffee for afters. Not what you'd call good cheer
But better than nothing – food, and talking shop.

The Deaf Home

In this cubit of air, are there words
Into which silence between the walls can fit?
Words written here, or read,
Are equal to that quietness.
Intoxicating night, beyond the open window –

A melody comes, or doesn't, from outside,
Staying out, like the night. Nothing steps in here,
In this silence which is not muteness, but deafness,
no one talks to me, no one gets an answer.
On the radio – the desert radio –
Unearthly voices, talking of nothing. Soundless,
They stay in the corner, choked in sand.
A telephone buzz. *Hallo* – and then the silence.
A second time. Yes? Was it you who didn't speak
A minute ago? A silence from the receiver,
And harder to bear, a silence after replacing it.
I try to speak to myself alone
But words don't enter the room, they are stopping short
On the mouth's doorstep, like rotten blackberries they crumble.
I didn't teach the walls to talk,
They have taken in neither gentle nor highflown words,
Only the quiet, bouncing it back like echoes.
Here is the home of silence. Inside it,
I am the quietest guest –
At my table, in my bed, in my body.

My Uncle the People

I am not the people. My father wasn't either
With his silence, his strange clothes. Somewhere
His soul changed. Only his brother
With brilliant speech and eyes, is the people.
It's warm at uncle's, at the people's
It's warm. But uncle alone of the people
Acknowledges me, and looks on me
As one of his own. The rest not much. I look on the people
As my own, I feel their warmth, pleasant
Or heavy. The people don't look upon me as their own
With my silence, my strange clothes. Somewhere
My soul changed. Uncle takes me by the arm
And talks with me, like an equal.
We sit on the doorstep. There in the sun
The wheat is a golden sheen.

Have you got a doorstep, my own flesh and blood,
He asks me, in that sheen. I have as many stairs
As you like, though I'm close to the earth,
And few people, nowadays, bother with a doorstep,
Even for their own house, only a threshold
The door will close on –
The people sit on a bench
In the foreground, or look in the window.
I have a bench there as well, next to the pump.
But a doorstep is different, uncle insists,
Worryingly. While we sit like that
We are inside and outside both, with our feet on the ground,
Our beam-ends too. I complain to my uncle –
When I wake up, I want my first step
To be on firm ground. I learnt that from ancient times.
But do the people pass by your house
And how do you get on with them, he asks me –
A difficult question. The people pass by the building,
They have no names, no faces.
It's the times we live in, uncle sighs.
Then we sit a while longer, the earth
Confirming us, a draught from the house at our backs.

The Morning Cut

Into my opened eyes
A heavenly blueness rushes. Light
Brightens the curtains. Behind them
White roofs of buildings there again, under the sky.
I have to feel sorry
That blue buildings, bringing the sky nearer,
Didn't do the trick instead.
Still, the world is in place again,
Passing the daily screen-test,
Almost. Something remains unclear
In the lingering sleep-world.
A riddle – that presence
In the leftover dream,
Why did it call me by someone else's name?

There, it will tell me. There, in the instant,
The waking dream –
If ever I woke. I open my eyes
And the sky stares blindingly in at once.
I will stand up, flex
My biceps. A day thrown open –
It will receive me, once again,
The everyday guest.

Cold Storage

At zero minus ten
The soul shrinks deeper into itself,
Goes quiet under the coat,
Shamming dead by the snow jaw.
I bear it home within me,
Timidly, over the bridge.
And suddenly, screams and laughter –
Another soul! The laughter
Splashes over me, like dirty water
Thrown by a redcoated passer-by.
(And her eyes were shining
As she looked right through me
There on the icebound bridge,
A look blown away now
Like snow off the frozen railings.
And her handbag – she held it
To herself, like no woman
Ever held a child…)
                              Even now
She is opening the door to her flat,
Going in, unfolding her sheets,
Like me, for hibernation.

Saturday Idyll

Is life worth living?
The answer, this Saturday, is yes.
The beggar on the bridge,
My first connection today,
Examined bits of change in her hand –
May God give you joy!
I sat in the rattletrap carrying me
As far as the cemetery. Morning sun
Flattered its bodywork, more flashily
Than anywhere else. In the black soil
Where happy tulips sprouted, in twin rows,
Like a miniature cornfield,
I plunged my hands.
                    Five fingers –
Enough to dig that patch of land,
The scented garden, by the house of the departed.
Cemetery visits – not too bad. They come and go,
My fellow beings,
On holidays, on any days.

On the way back, a different beggar
Waited for me on the bridge. Extracting alms
She showed me her tiny baby –
An apple for the baby! Better than I did,
She knew what was in my bag.
And straight away, the baby took to the apple
Like a vast nipple.
                    Then, with a melancholic friend,
I broke the bread of midday.
Life doesn't seem to agree with him
But it doesn't show up on his photos, about which
He worries no longer. Or maybe it does show,
I don't know. One of them
I rearranged on the wall for a long time
After his departure. To the little girl
In the photograph, I said sweet nothings,
Just like every day – *It's all right, it's worth it,*
It's better to be alive, on a day like this.

HADŽEM HAJDAREVIĆ

Translations by RUTH PADEL / ANTONELA GLAVINIĆ

Hadžem Hajdarević was born in 1956 in Kruševo, northern Montenegro, near Foča in Bosnia. After completing his studies at the famous Gazi Husrevbegova Medresa (an Islamic secondary school) in Sarajevo, he studied Serbo-Croat literatures at Sarajevo University. His poetry is imbued with the Islamic culture of the Balkans, and characterised by an intense linguistic verve and musicality. He now teaches Bosnian language and literature at a medresa in Sarajevo, where he remained during the siege. He also writes fiction and criticism, and edits the weekly current affairs journal *Liljan (Fleur-de-Lis)*.

Main publications: *The Shifting of Shores* (1981), *Which Noah's Ark?* (1987), *The Living Waters* (1990), and *Subterranean Poems* (1995).

Keeping Guard in Dobrinja

Why am I calling you
when you're closer to me than I am?
You've got my eyes in your hand.
You're my pulse, the way my own blood wells
in a wound. The body might forget you a moment
but the soul, a cage-bird
starving for oxygen, pick-pecks the veins.

Between good and evil, and the girl
who cannot tell sin from her shame
we only know the morning flush of terror,
rock-chasms between ways of knowing God.

You shudder me into words. They bless
me and I hide in them, afraid.
You breathe in me poems from your milky chest
and white teeth. Poems about a spider, about clay,

about a face gasping for air. Your fingers find
and shape me all the time.
I'm always with you; and with the One
who sent you here. My estuary.
My riverbank. Your eagle eye's
watching me, Death, as I watch dead windows
and breathe out loud in dead night.

The Voices Are Coming

Soldiers, and nights full of leaves.
I scrape off insomnia like sugar
from the bottom of a burnt-out pan.
Girls' screams bury the day in elm-flutter,
elm-drift. There was nothing we could do to avoid

what came, or wanted to come. Wolves on shift
in the hills
howled at moonslivers, moonrakings,
moondust. The whole chaos world
converged on the changing moon.

We float leaf-words to the ground
and gaze in each other.
Who got left out of the song?
Whose are these prayers
leaking from open wounds, whose soul

lapping poisonous wine? In the smoke
of Azrail, angel of death,
we sat, you and I.
December's dog barked at the gate.
In the house was a dead key and mortice

plus long, steppy dark.
The bride from the plain brought
such unreal hands to the hills.
We didn't say a word. We watched her
at otherworld work. Trees fizzed with lice.

We waited for the call
to start down the slope
but look, we're still here –
where your eyes ache
with longing to find mine.

Death was a trophy aquarium, a jewelly jet
of water where shadows dissolved
to a warm
mother-calm: a ship
on its journey to Ahyret.*

* *Ahyret:* the other world, death.

October 31st

Like gardens in Rilke's 'Autumn',
the war's wilting everyone's face.
Everything sinks to its first tenderness
then snaps back at us wrinkled and hard.
Every morning we wash off giant's sweat
that falls from our clothes, the sleepy clothes
made by those who kissed and loved us
long ago. At that moment every move we make
is our first and our last.

The window's awash with blood and the door is dead.
Skin's peeled off the wall. October lies in bed
like a beast with Bosnian women.
And I writhe naked, barefoot on every leaf.
There's no going back on the wing of child-dreams.
The veil on everything I chase
glows whiter. Colours blaze
transparent as drunk water, refugees lying out
on soft ground...

We could have met October on the wind's upland,
or in our own placenta – as we met war,
as we meet the hand of the sculptor who hefts
us and blacks us. If we fall
it's someone else's dark. How, after that, can we
be an upright pole, or grow bark
like a tree? How be strong, when October's deaf
to every voice huckled into its ear,
drop by translucent drop?

Pregnant Girl

You feel sea-murmur, a buzzing April *galop*.
The waves are rumbustious greyhounds
but you are a full-fig garden.
Turn your eyes deepsea to the crimson-
and-tequila-sunrise rocks
where south wind swells the bellies of the sails.

The rippled-snakeskin wind is a black sailor
with a silver ear-hoop. Don't break out
in shame. Don't get any nearer pure blue.
Touch wild roots at high tide
as the sea grows gentler with itself and you,
and splashes your ankles. St George's hour

ticks over louder, for you. Young rain falls
on the softsilk membrane
where scarlet angels pucker
the umbilical cord.
As if you'd made love with a dolphin
in a sailor's dream; or mine.

The Camp: and Her Brother's Death Foreseen

In the dark we're all beautiful and dead.
We're empty houses squatted in by bats.
We're cages for winged dogs. In the dark
you die little bit by little bit.

All this was in your broken sentences
as they closed the dead city's eyes.
I think more, now, of your theory of the dark.
'Is darkness the gas form of earth,
the thick gaze of the dead?'

Even you – like you hardly existed.
You rooted in the womb of everything,
every word, thought or sound.
All I remember resists. Public confessions

razoring the inner membrane of the eye.
The camps – those souls in the ash-shaft,
ash-tree. Years have passed
since you were the birch-tree's leaflight,
your taproots trawling my body.

I can't bear the restless rose
or myself, or the dark that eats me up.
I keep still, longing for *kudret*:
the time bomb and clock-tick of God.

Deserted Ship in Alexandria

You can only fill emptiness with looking.
If you want the future or past
try a glamorous antique smile, or a drowning
hallo. Try crumbling tiny lumps of earth
between your fingers, mashing the centuries.
Say your childhood wasn't here
in front of the house, all thick boots on mud,
the white bird under the roof
and those snowclouds of feathers. You heard

cicadas in the garden, shaking your curls.
Willow-wind flickered through every live thing.
Now you're quiet,
a fish in your own eye's well.
When the hour-glass sifts through the bones
you'll know why everything you see
bursts like a pomegranate spilling its seed
in the years, the caravan of years;
and why this ship sinks

in new memory. Remember each shape,
every new silhouette to its edge.
Anything may be the key, may heal
the emptiness we spread
to some later-on moment. Everything's already
been crumbled
by somebody looking, somebody
teaching us about the bride, about the rose
that's been burning these thousand years.

Trout Evening

April blew into the nursery bubbles
under algae-swirled slabbing

and the secret shapes beneath
agreed to partition –

to the new presences secretly swelling
between murmurs that go on and go on.

In all this relief of veins and sand,
a trout is getting ready for spawning:

the little connecting bands
hum in the delicate isthmus, the river's secret calm.

The egg-sac gushes a hundred-strong chorus.
What'll happen

when the waters freeze? God! Will it be
just blood, slime and mucus

when I lean over with the bait, with all this blind
hunger? The evening's clotting on the hook,

the little mouth contracts. The riverbank's inlaid
with silver patina. This is the panic-trail,

where cicadas help my darling
dreamweave me a shirt from the fog.
My trout gives a final ice-shudder, a yawn.
Day breaks. Look! A window! Someone's eternity gone!

Any moment now
these below-water fields will get me

instead of the trout. Will water flow
in my eyes?

My Animal

I often take my animal to the mountains.
There's more juniper, there's less damp there.
Angels start fires. The mountain-air's full

of mare's milk. I show it
the thickest grass, springs
frothing from the jugular. Lairs to lie up in.

At evening I take it down to the rivers: to the villages
and wine feasts. All the way back
I pick flowers and make masks.

If I speak at all, I howl in its language.
I introduce it to everything that might
touch its heart. I ride it when it wants me to.

I carry it over crags till I'm almost dead,
till my soul's a rushlight
in the nose. I am its justice-scales, its good

sea foam; its moonflood and wild soprano rose.
But it slivers its tongue in my throat
and draws blood.

Gottfried Benn* in Café Sarajevo 94

The candle melts, a frightened boy-soldier on guard,
till a generator mashes the ears...

Long greasy hair
dribbles over the edges of smoke. Next to it – look,

– toothless jokes about a bad Bosnian,
and a twist-belly devoured by jealousy, by ulcers.

Spectacles are pouring out vodka. Here are crutches of maple
lolling about at my table. A pair of knees

buckles beneath a nicotine-
yellow moustache. And there is a hat against a wall,

spying on commerce between
warmed-up dentures and runny saliva.

Tired eyelids are singing backnumbers from the hills
of Dalmatia. Seventeen-year-old leggings lope in

with the Tuborg beer. That jaw, slurping brandy
through a straw, has been operated on. There is a thigh

whose shell-fragments flirt with a just-lighted joint.
We must get away! get abroad! Grey hairs on a bending head

gather courage to touch – what? a breastcancer? Oh –
a new brand! TB's rubbing slumberous eyes

in its own cigarette smoke. The fiddle-bow keeps playing tunes
while accordion-blood

rushes screaming over the floor. Should I stand up
and start something? Scream, or strip naked?

The leggings and darksweat young blouse
are hallooing instead. 'The hat has been stabbed!

In the shoulders, the neck...' I go out very slowly, full
of the pus of the camp. After me

stagger two lonely wristveins, well swathed from the world,
that are going to get slashed

in precisely
one hour and a half...

* *Gottfried Benn:* 18th-century German poet.

New York New York

Someone met you halfway
between life and death. Met his own
wicked whitewater rapids, foaming
through where he was born.
All things whirl into and out
of the riverbed, into tomorrow.

You've silk-wrapped all that:
the dove-breath, the family white bird
you inherited so long ago. Afraid
of the estuary coming too soon,
you hold to the bottom, the home.

I'd like you to fountain, flow up, change
the groove of the rapids
where hearts get hammered and torn.
Swallows flow over grey houses while terror
and horror have moused themselves home
in the ground.

Someone will see, but they won't understand
the smell, the mud-movement, God's
gorgeous and whirlpool ingredients;
won't see why I've become
a pebble in Babylon's flood,
that damburst of language and voice...

VOJKA DJIKIĆ

Translations by CHRIS AGEE / ANTONELA GLAVINIĆ

Vojka Djikić was born in 1932 in Mrkonjić Grad, northern Bosnia, and studied literature at Belgrade University. She was poetry editor for Sarajevo radio and TV from 1973 to the outbreak of the war, and also edited the journal *The Third Programme* produced by Sarajevo Radio. *Joie de vivre*, stoicism and an apprehension of historical calamity are fused in a poetry of brevity and atmosphere. She is a professional translator of French and Algerian literature, and continues to live in Sarajevo, where she remained during the siege.

Main publications: *Poems* (1966), *The Weaver of Winds* (1987), and *Ash-Wednesday* (1997).

Summer Lament

I know never again shall I stand
at the door of St Nicholas Church
in a white linen dress
and watch the light go down

waves
obscure the view

Never again will I stand
at the portals of the cathedral
and watch the seagulls
under the antique sky of Korcula

winds
scatter us

Tonight we hardly suspect it
idling on the stone square
full of gulls and girls
who lament a summer

[1990]

VOJKA DJIKIĆ

Persistent Ancestors

Time and Night
those persistent tricksters
stocking the wild reserves
with ancestors who wait
a thousand years for the right
to new existence
and newer crimes

In an age without memory
shadow-columns marching
are muddying the truth

That long before
I was born
some persistent ancestor
flourished the gospel of the Book
and with it cursed me

A Guest May Come

Hold on tight to me
And we'll find the way home
There the fire's still burning
And in the corners
Books lie open
That ought to be read
And the garden's there to dig
The roses to prune
Thus it was said
When we mend the roof
And paint the red door red
A guest may come

Almost a Life

Grilled fish
            and a jug of homemade wine
            F and R
                        almost a life
            returning through the moonlight
                        towards
            the hard reality of dreams
            the sky's weight
                        on the naked body

Deserted Campsites

We gutter in memory
                        like deserted campsites
Cheerful yet sombre
we must bid farewell to the body
                        which assumes the colour and shape
of the earth

Here in this poem there is no room
for those I love

We must bid farewell to the words
which have betrayed us

The campsites gutter
Ghosts are disguised as valleys
                        full of fog
where mountains and rivers
stand arrested
                        before our empty homes

HAMDIJA DEMIROVIĆ

Translations by CHARLES SIMIC

Hamdija Demirović was born in 1953 in Sarajevo, and studied comparative literature at Sarajevo University. His first two collections, in 1976 and 1978, quickly established him as one of the most widely acclaimed young poets in Yugoslavia. In his poems, 'erudition sings', as one critic has said of him; and a recurrent theme is the *exposé* of the world as it is, rather than as it has been presented. Despite his small output, his work has had a major influence on Bosnian poetry, especially among a generation of poets which first appeared in the eighties. He lived in Belgrade between 1985 and 1992, when he emigrated to the Netherlands, where he has lived since. He is also a distinguished translator of poetry from English, notably volumes of Pound, Whitman and Stevens, as well as lesser selections of Yeats, Auden and Owen. *Twenty-five Poems*, a selection of his work translated by Charles Causley, was published in 1980 by the Keepsake Press, England. He now divides his time between Amsterdam and The Hague, where he works for the International War Crimes Tribunal for the Former Yugoslavia.

Main publications: *Secrets Revealed* (1976), *Chimera and Reasons* (1978), and *The Name in the Mountain* (forthcoming).

Anti-Mauberley

I

Not three – but thirty years almost
He strove to elevate and 'resuscitate'.
Everything flew so slowly, slowly…
Drop by drop, given that the milk

Had dried up in the teat. Our Mother
(Didn't you know?) was a witch.
The oldest one, she named 'Pater'
Without thinking, poor widow.

He understood finally that in savage land
It doesn't pay to 'give peace a chance',
So that lilies in their bloom
He couldn't tell apart from the acorns.

His birthplace became Troy.
His true Penelope was not Flaubert
But grave mounds without end.
Seas he didn't cross, the dead he didn't bury.

So now, what 'curl' and 'numbers'
Can he sing shipwrecked on the rocks?
While victims sob, press seashells to his ears,
So as not to hear, not to see?

II

No, the age did not demand
An image of its 'accelerated grimace'.
As for something of 'modern grace' –
Not a chance.

Of the 'revery of the inward gaze',
No hint. Only mass movements
Where band music is the rule
And the classics are in paraphrase.

The age demanded absolutely nothing.
Neither 'alabaster' nor 'prose kinema'.
Nor 'sculpture' of plays in rhyme.
Savagery suited them just fine.

III

If only by some luck Sappho's
'Pianola' had replaced 'barbitos'.
Here accordion and flute held sway
And good taste was disdained.

Neither 'Christ', 'Dionysius' nor 'Phallus',
Just plain old godless slaughter.
Where Ariel loses his pride,
There's no point to sacrifice.

Yes, 'all flows' chez Heraclitus…
Here nothing budges.
Time makes stalactites.
Les fleurs du mal is all that grows.

IV

Some, in any case, 'fought'.
Some, perhaps, 'believing'.
But never 'pro domo'.
Never 'dolce et decorum'.

All quick to arm
Out of a fear not to appear weak,
For the love of slaughter – the real kind,
Not for the sake of any 'learning',
Neither before nor after.

*

Myriads died, truly,
But certainly not the 'best'.
The toothless old bitch
The 'botched civilisation',

Bad as it is, will outlive yet
All our drivel and prattle.

'For the heap of broken statues',
'For a few thousand battered books',
Nobody ever died, buddy boy:

We sent someone to kingdom come
For two handfuls of gold teeth,
A pitcher of beer and slivovitz.

V

As he passed *l'an trentiesme de son age*,
The 'age demanded' slight, whispery prose:
Hounds, gardens and lies were the fashion;
The age demanded and got its pause.

Now as his fourth decade wanes,
He feels unable to fulfill the call;
The lyric masquerade bores him;
He'd rather find his lair somewhere.

Pastoral Divertissement

At times, it happens, we have a premonition
Of an idyllic landscape with a clearing, a forest,
A village in the background and the inevitable spring
Of cold mountain water with an occasional worn water wheel.
And immediately afterwards, at the pleasure of our assassin fantasy,
Or some cannabis-like excitement of our minds,
The spring turns crystal, crumbled into thousands
Of teeny quartz particles that grind each other –
As they shatter under the bearded wheel!
Some float in the ozone-rich air and glitter
Under the blue sun in the orange sky. Purple
Meadow, breathes with its every grass leaf as it parts
And tears into thinner and thinner blades,
So that the entire sheath looks plastic,
Like a spike-studded bed of a lecherous fakir.
And the sheep are pink marble statues wearing rubber boots.
Anyway, a whole cluster of yellow clarinets
Comes into being, glistening under the rays
Of the splintered sunlight, (each one in its own corner
Sharp and metallic in the azimuthal projection of the sky),
And an entire downpour of flywheels, as a result,
Bubbles on the boiling surfaces of the earth...
Pinkish drapery evens itself out and tightens
Into the pregnant skin of a drum, into the mad curtain
Of an orchestra hall with the cacophony
Of unharmonised violins behind it. Black
Tailcoat and the conductor's baton tune
The orchestra for a debauched pastoral symphony.

Some of the Secrets Are Out

Under this divine, omniscient eye,
Of which we have only a presentiment,
terrifying things are hidden.
The night bird, Owl, is only a small
part of that metaphor of horror.

Myriads of stars and maelstroms
of new galaxies come afterwards.
I know the stars are sticky and suggest
oil colours with a tendency to drip.
That's why there are comets and long-tailed
swarms. Their plunging in the depths
of the cosmos doesn't carry any hint
of free choice. Like drops on a frozen
background of a dark windowpane,
some suddenly slip and hurry toward
their own perdition.

Leaving behind always a trail of light.

Religion

My god is Chance; I'm his servant.
My calling is scribe; debt collector.
I can do all sorts of things – both good and evil;
I sing inspired without loosing my foothold.

I said, I have wings on my feet.
I dispense gifts, also love to receive them.
Clever thoughts I strew over the planet.
All the space cadets dance for me.
Step by step, I feel nothing – I fly,
The speed in the vein freezes the blood.

Don't touch me, brother, my Giant protects me –
Let no word reach his ear.
You don't know what it means to be pinned down.
How sweet the defeat in my shoulder-blades.

He is not full of wrath, like your god.
Nothing alive steps on his foot
(Except at times when Fate trips him
When he's tipsy, so crushes someone).

MILJENKO JERGOVIĆ

FROM **Sarajevo Marlboro** (1994)

Translated by STELA TOMAŠEVIĆ

Beard

Juraj's head lay in the mud like an empty dish into which the rain-drops fell. But the soldiers marched past without giving him a second look. A few steps away his neighbour Šimun, who was digging a two-yard trench, stared at the iridescent clay with a peculiar feeling of emptiness in the back of his neck and also perhaps with a kind of premonition, as opposed to fear, that soon his own head would be cut off and used for slopping-out as in a prison latrine. Once in a while he glanced out of the corner of his eye at the trench which Juraj had been digging an hour before. Šimun imagined a person measuring the hole through which Juraj's brain had seeped on to the ground. He admired its geometrical shape and reflected to himself that such a thing could have been moulded by a skilful potter render-ing God's creation with ease as if it were nothing but dust and water.

Dinka came with two other women just before nightfall. They were led up the hill by gloomy bearded men in uniform. One of the soldiers turned over Juraj's body with his foot and mumbled out of the side of his mouth, 'Is this him?' Dinka nodded and then looked away. The women departed immediately without glancing back, leaving Juraj in his new position. Now it was possible to see his life-less staring eyes and the tiny hole in his forehead. His arms were folded on his chest, and his mouth was open, as if he had seen the trail of a jet plane in the sky for the first time. His look suggested that he was about to ask timidly, 'What is that?' Šimun would have liked to go over to the body in order to close his friend's eyes – any-thing to stop the raindrops welling there like tears – but he wasn't sure how the soldiers would react, and who knows if Juraj would have looked any better with his eyes shut, or what kind of impres-sion it would create and how much it would continue to haunt the prisoner who was still alive and digging.

Before his capture Juraj had spent four months hiding in cellars, refusing to abandon hope that one day something unexpected would happen to make the Chetniks go away or perhaps he dreamed of suddenly waking up one morning in a strange country far away, or, at any rate, on the other side of the river. Every day he was visited by Dejan, a poet friend from the Writers' Club, who had taken to wearing a Serbian cap and letting his unkempt beard grow down to his navel. Dejan was permanently drunk – in honour of the war. Sometimes he gave Juraj a hug and whispered (or burped) in his ear that he intended to sort things out and that the longed-for day would soon arrive when Juraj could once again walk through Sarajevo without shame or fear, like an honourable and decent man. But drunks have an unfortunate habit of suddenly changing their outlook on the world. And so, having consoled his friend, Dejan would often go on to observe in the same tone of voice how excellent it would be if he the Serbian poet were to use his knife to slit the throat of Juraj the Croatian poet right here and now on the shagpile carpet. Out loud he began to imagine Juraj's death rattle or the blood seeping across the room, or perhaps the fetid smell of his soul escaping from his body and wafting from wall to wall in search of an open window. The monologue usually came to an end with Dejan imagining the ode to slaughter he would write to commemorate killing his friend. Juraj never rose to the bait. He just kept his mouth shut and smiled innocuously like a lamb. Dinka, on the other hand, looked petrified as she stood in the corner of the room, yearning for Dejan to leave and for the next chapter in her life to begin.

Dejan soon got bored anyway. On the way out he'd shake hands with Dinka as well as Juraj, and leave yelling, 'Your Dejo's looking out for you, so don't worry! He'll save you, goddamit! A true friend ain't just a button, see, and his wife's not a zip, either!'

As soon as he'd gone, Dinka would begin to cry, and so Juraj would stroke her shoulder with the tips of his fingers, because there was nothing to be said. The couple had a sneaking suspicion that one day Dejan would honour one or the other of his promises, and yet it was hard to know if he was more likely to rescue them from murderers or to deliver the fatal blows himself.

One day a gang of bearded men whom they didn't know burst into the cellar. These anonymous thugs proceeded to beat up Dinka and to 'draft' Juraj into what they called 'the labour platoon'. As a result, he spent months on the front line, only ten yards or so from the Bosnian line, digging trenches. Often he would recognise a soldier on the opposite side by the colour of his eyes or the way he walked. Out of delight he would open his mouth to speak to his comrades, but they just ducked their heads, so he was left having imaginary conversations with their gun barrels. At first he panicked in case the warring armies opened fire, but as time went on he came to realise that the killing would not begin unexpectedly. There would have to be a kind of advance warning, he was sure, a portent in the sky, or perhaps a dawn chorus prophesying death, in order to distinguish the day of slaughter from the others that had preceded it. Dejan continued to visit Dinka. He brought her food and claimed drunkenly that only he could save Juraj, and that he knew Juraj would do the same for him if, heaven forbid, the tables were turned and the Ustashas were defeating the Chetniks. Dinka merely nodded her head, looking forlorn, so Dejan tried to get round her by telling jokes.

One day he asked her, 'Tell me, Dinka, would you let me fuck you if I managed to get Juraj out of the shit?'

Dinka looked away, her lips trembling with fury, but she remained silent.

'Listen, sweetheart, I didn't say I wanted to or anything. I'm just curious – would you let me? Don't you see that I have to know what kind of person you are and how fond you are of Juraj? Take me, for example. I couldn't be more fond of him than I already am. If I reckoned it'd save his bacon, I'd let you fuck me. Honest! Without a second thought. So it's really a question of who cares more about your husband you or me?'

Dejan left the house volunteering to go to Pale, if necessary, in order to save Juraj. He warned her not to get upset about his teasing. We're human beings, after all, not animals, he said.

Dinka couldn't help remembering that conversation as she was coming down the hill with the other women after identifying Juraj's body. She was still trying to comprehend that her Juraj was no more, and that nothing was left of him except a hollow skull. As she wiped her eyes she saw Dejan beaming at her in the distance. He was running up the hill and waving a piece of paper above his head. Dinka prayed that he would just vanish into thin air. He stopped in the middle of a sentence but she couldn't bear to look at him or to listen to what he was saying about headquarters... orders from the very top... the real important people... the necessary papers... All she could think was, 'How on earth does he wash that beard – does he shampoo it or does he just wash his face in the morning like everybody else?'

The Photograph

'Our idea of love is not letting other people steal your woman.'
DUŠKO TRIFUNOVIĆ

I don't know what it's like anywhere else, but in Europe it's like this: Rick is unhappy because Ilse loves Laszlo. He knows that she loves him too, and yet she remains faithful to Laszlo. Rick wishes she'd be faithful to him instead – because it's not enough to know that she loves him. No doubt you have heard and read the same story, with a few variations, a thousand times. The key to true love is faithfulness. You don't need to think about it much – it is taken for granted. Mind you, if it wasn't for faithfulness, there probably wouldn't be any unhappiness in love. Nor any happiness either.

Senka and Mašo were often cited in the neighbourhood as love's young dream. She was unable to have any children, but he didn't hold that against her as other Balkan husbands might have done. Senka worked in the Post Office and Mašo was a plumber. She always used to refer to him as 'my Mašo', and he to her as 'my Senka'. Their story would not have been of any interest if the war had not broken out. We don't usually find stories about long and happy relationships very interesting.

As soon as the shelling began Mašo joined the Territorial Army. Senka was not very pleased about this, but she realised that there was no other way of preserving their one-bedroom Eden. The very thought of leaving town scared her. A different place would mean different circumstances; it would be a story involving different characters.

One day a strange man in uniform with muddy boots knocked on the door. He hugged Senka and whispered to her that Mašo had been killed. He left a paper bag with Mašo's possessions on the table – a hanky, the case for his spectacles and his wallet. After the first few days of mourning, which are usually more ceremonious than sorrowful, and which demand a certain presence of mind to avoid the compassionate gazers who thrive on any sign of tears, Senka took out all the things that had been returned to her instead of Mašo. She touched each object in turn and finally opened the wallet. Inside she found fifty Deutschmarks – an amount that any cautious man perhaps would always carry with him – and odd scraps of paper with phone numbers and notes about plumbing. In the little plastic window was a photograph of Senka. The only purpose of the plastic window is to give a glimpse of your intimate life to strangers at supermarket checkouts. But the wallet also had a secret invisible compartment. Senka peeked into it and found a photograph of an unknown woman. On the back was written, 'Always yours, Mirsada'. The handwriting was flowery with many loops. The next day Senka told the whole neighbourhood what those 'bastards from the brigade had done to her'. Angrily, then bitterly and in the end tearfully, she showed the incriminating photograph to the women, who tut-tutted and shook their heads. They consoled her as she was leaving their houses and then immediately began to gossip about her. On the whole, everyone, except of course Senka, was pleased to discover that Mašo hadn't been a saint. They secretly considered her pitiful for having revealed so publicly her shame, which she didn't even acknowledge.

When, a fortnight or so later, the boys from the brigade came with a parcel for the wife of a dead comrade, she refused to open the door to them. She shouted at them through the door, making various threats and curses. When Senka declined the army handout, most of the neighbours just assumed that she had gone mad already. They pulled at the soldiers' sleeves, trying to get them to leave the parcel, so that they could pass it on to Senka when she calmed down.

As time went by, the widespread compassion turned to ridicule. Nobody any longer wanted to hear her story about the inserted photograph, which had gradually acquired a thousand twists. On the other hand, Senka was always trying to come up with a story that would clear Mašo's name. Each day she added new details. Yesterday's reasons disappeared in a flash before today's uncertainties. But the story about love's young dream always triumphed in the end. Senka believed that she had to sacrifice everything, including her sanity. In this war-stricken town, deprived of hope, Senka had nothing to cling to but her story.

I don't know what happened after that because I left Sarajevo. But perhaps the ending is not very important. Once again, faithfulness has been confirmed as the axiom of love, as something that is more important than love itself. But in any case, what transcends even the bounds of this story is our need to create a fable, or a context, to make sense of life and thus give it a purpose.

The people who write about the war in Bosnia without any thought of personal gain, or any wish to clamber over the bodies of the living and the dead in order to achieve success – a select few, in other words – are actually quite similar to Senka. Without any profit to themselves or others, they bravely seek to preserve an image of a world that has been shattered. Sometimes their unflinching descriptions or honest reports, not to mention their uncompromising points of view, offend public opinion. It is not unknown for such writings to be condemned as national treason by Orthodox believers. But in fact they are only vain attempts to discover a truth, a reason to exist. At a time when just about everything else has been lost or destroyed, faithfulness is the only thing left to believe in. When the time comes to write the history of Bosnia, only people like Senka will resist its lies.

The Library

You hear the whistle over your head. It's followed by the odd moment of suspense, and then below, somewhere in the city, there's an explosion. You can always see the spot clearly from your window. At first there's a tall, thin column of dust which turns to smoke and flames. You wait a few minutes to work out what sort of building it is. If the fire is slow and lazy, it means that the burning flat belongs to some poor people. If it bursts into a huge, blue fireball, then it's somebody's nicely decorated attic with panelled walls burning. If it burns unremittingly, then the flames must be coming from the apartment of a wealthy shop-owner, full of massive antique furniture. But if the flame suddenly shoots up, wild and uncontrollable, like the hair of Farrah Fawcett, and disappears even more rapidly, allowing the wind to spread paper ash over the city, that means somebody's private library has just burned down. As you witnessed many such vigorous fires over the months and years of shelling, you got to feel that the foundations of Sarajevo must have been made out of books. And even if they weren't, you'd like to say, as you stroke the bound volumes on your shelves, that the city still contains many books that have not yet been destroyed.

In any private library most of the books have not been read. No doubt you bought this one or that one because of its cover or the author's name, or simply because the smell of the paper appealed to you. You pick up such a book often in the early days, open it, read a few lines and then put it back. After a while you forget about the book, or else you look at it from a distance with mild disgust. You have often wanted to take it to the nearest public library and to give it to somebody, just to get rid of the thing in some way, but you were never able to do so. It will always remind you of your tendency to hoard useless things, and will soon transform itself, in a painful burning moment, into a host of other memories. All those unnecessary and unread books will prove to be a burden when it's time to leave them behind. You may almost come to understand the fire's rapture as it engulfs similar books around the city.

There are a few books which you have not opened since childhood. They remind you of a time when you still hadn't learned to scan the pages, to read from the top left-hand corner to the bottom right. These are probably the only books you have really enjoyed in your life. All the best children's stories had an unhappy ending which didn't teach you anything, except that sadness is a place where fiction becomes more important than reality. In John Huston's film *The Dead*, a woman bursts into tears and is unable to say why. As you watched the film, you thought that this was in fact the way life is – and you too felt like crying.

There are even fewer books that you imagined you'd always carry with you. When you read one for the first time, you'd try and postpone the ending. Later on, you found them exciting in both content and appearance. But you will have to leave them behind, just like all the others, with the bitter conviction that not only in this city, but also in the world at large, a book's natural state of aggregation is fire, smoke and ash. Somebody in the future may find this pathetic, but for you, especially when you end up in other cities where bookshops still exist, Farrah Fawcett's flaming hair will always be the plain truth. The only thing that burns better, more beautifully and more thoroughly than a book is a manuscript.

With the illusion of a private library also vanishes the illusion of a *bibliotheca*, or civilisation of books. Its very name, which is just a Greek word, like any other, but which is, for you, tied to the name of the Holy Scriptures, was enough to make you a believer. But, as they burned, disappearing irrevocably one after the other, you stopped believing that there was any purpose in a book's existence. Or perhaps the only one to have worked out their purpose was that Sarajevan author and bibliophile who, instead of using expensive firewood, warmed his fingers last winter on the flames of Dostoevsky, Tolstoy, Shakespeare, Cervantes... As a result of so many deliberate and accidental fires, a new kind of person has been created, a person who has come bitterly to understand how things go and who, as a result, would coolly watch flames rising from the Louvre and not even reach out for a glass of water. There's no point in not letting a fire swallow up things that human indifference has already destroyed. The beauty of Paris or London is only an alibi for the criminals who have allowed Warsaw, Dresden, Vukovar and Sarajevo to disappear. But even if they hadn't ceased to exist, they would have become places inhabited by people who even in peacetime were

ready to evacuate, who were prepared to abandon their books.
In this world, as it is, there is one basic rule; Zuko Džumhur
mentioned it when he was thinking about Bosnia, and it relates to
the two suitcases that you always have packed in the hall. All your
possessions and all your memories have to fit into them. Everything
outside is already lost. There is no point in looking for reasons or
meanings or excuses. They are just a burden, like memories. There is
nothing left but to return the books you have borrowed in the past,
trying to avoid or to miss out the ones you were given as presents,
and the others you've made a note about to send to friends who live
elsewhere, so that those books would not be engulfed in flames –
or, at any rate, not until the day the world returns to the condition it
was in a few million years ago.

You can never list or recall the private libraries that have burned
down in Sarajevo. And why should you? But the fate of the Sarajevo
University Library, its famous city hall, whose books took a whole
night and day to go up in flames, will be remembered as the fire to
end all fires, a last mythical celebration of ash and dust. It happened,
after a whistle and an explosion, almost exactly a year ago. Perhaps
the same date you're reading this [25 August]. Gently stroke your
books, dear stranger, and remember they are dust.

Miljenko Jergović was born in Sarajevo in 1966. A poet and journalist, he
writes for the daily *Oslobodjenje*. *Sarajevo Marlboro* is his first book.

HUSEIN TAHMIŠČIĆ

Translations by JOHN HARTLEY WILLIAMS

Husein Tahmiščić was born in 1931 in Sarajevo, and took a degree in philosophy and Yugoslav literatures at Sarajevo University. For nearly two decades he was the editor of *Izraz* (Expression), one of the best literary reviews in postwar Yugoslavia, as well as co-founder and editor of *Kniga i Svijet* (Books and the World), *Danas* (Today) and *Odjek* (Echo). The recipient of many awards, he is also a prolific author of essays, criticism, radio drama, short stories and children's literature. He has edited several anthologies of Bosnian poetry, the last being *Subterranean River* (1983). Firmly rooted in the rich modernist and surrealist traditions of Yugoslav poetry, many of his poems are written (unusually for a Bosnian) in the 'ekavski' or Serbian version of the language. Now blind, he returned to Sarajevo in 1996 from Prague, where he had spent the latter part of the war.

Main publications: *Life Traveller* (1954), *Prelude for Builders* (1958), *Builders* (1960), *The Recaptured City* (criticism, 1961), *Where Is It Tolling Now?* (1964), *Choice and Speech* (criticism, 1964), *School of Love* (1965), *Selected Poems* (1968), *Sarajevo Chronicle* (criticism, 1972) and *Anabasis* (1986).

Prague Meditation
(21 August 1968)

It's happened again. Summer's over.
Its tracks are being hidden; the word
so difficult to say
is being gulped down,
by a burning, opening mouth of earth,
under the dull cloak of an autumn sky.

Yes, it's happened. Summer's gone.
I walk through the ruins, through everything
                    that one day will be restored,
through memories which crush me and give me hope,
through this poem, surrendering its place to anxiety,
through everything which lives, struggles, hopes,
on the banks of the Viltava.

Summer gave way to exhaustion.
It's here in the harvest of my own thoughts.
My mind is occupied with things
that have discoloured reverie, put mundane worry to flight,
here: where I was thrown into the daylight world,
here: where love brought me, made me put down roots.

It's over. Summer is departing
from a world full of cuckoos' eggs.
And that's me, a wakeful man on his own doorstep,
startled from a tranquil dream by force:

a steel bullet has entered his heart –
a steel bullet and his heart is melting it slowly.
There's no other choice.

In this summer's vanishing, friends,
the lawbooks of heart and mind
are all we have left.
And, of course, this walk
through a world of suffering,
encompassed by a total darkness.
These thoughts are all I have.

You're Not a Man If You Don't Die
(on hearing the news of the death of Velimir Stojanović)

Let me tell you the shortest story
Let's shut our ears to those vampire professors
Let me tell you what the poets *really* meant
– *You're not a man if you don't die*

Let me read your palm and quiz your heart
Let's not applaud when they fiddle with the truth
Let me wash your eyes with light from the restless sky
– *You're not a man if you don't die*

Let me take down the seventh heaven and offer it to you
Let's not go willingly down any more garden paths
Let me put a candle in your head, open the door of the night
– *You're not a man if you don't die*

Let me bring peace to your innocent skull
Let me dust your sleep with dreams of icing sugar
Let me show you amazing vineyards that ripen and glow
- *You're not a man until you've died like one*

A Prayer Unfolded

The sky-blue of it, a flight of birds above the playground.
Our game streams up in the string of a blazing dragon-kite,
and fate is a peal of bells, a field of flowers,
the green coldness of a wreath.
Holding a wistful shell to our ear, an echo-less voice,
we hear marine whisperings, promising growth.
The sky's crown has its roots in the depths of the ocean

Open the circle of the game, fathers, it's playtime again.
Let's hold hands above the ashpile.
Beyond seven giant mountains and seven fat seas
the jokes are dancing in a wheel,
a white flower has broken its leg in the game,
and there the dragons are real –
the clouds ride, clinging to their own manes.

From here to the toys
there's no going back, you say,
but it's our game of hide and seek,
your silence of the playground.
A wise man showed us in a game
how to reach the sun –
and from the earth drawn back like a bow
muscles were released, bodies became arrows.
So spare us the lame excuses,
spare us the hypocrisies and fraud.
Can you see the eyes
in the loose sand blown across the schoolyard?
Can you see the children fashioned out of wind?
Can it be wrong to dance around the ashpile once again?
Return us to the toys, fathers, believe in the dream.
Who cares if your world is too narrow!
Be quiet. Watch. The game is about to start.

The Carousel

Wants to open the circle and depart
Wants to enter a bar full of girls and soldiers
Wants to listen attentively to that bickering and haggling
Wants to protest
Against the low price of circles
Against the routine of spinning round on a single pivot
Wants to start moving
In circles superior to itself
Wants above all
To be its own boss

But the curse of this world
Makes it stay put on the outskirts of town
Makes it spawn pennies and sixpences
Makes it spell consolation to childhood
And dream of that someday walk

Wreck

The air was perfumed the western sun had blossomed
Summer's clarity distilled its sweetness to a fruit
Oarsmen heaved, exhaled, their smooth strokes
Turned each sweaty heartbeat to propulsive unison
The calmness prophesied it the muscular harmony
Shrank to nothing suddenly rhythm's image cracked

Fate undid
The strength of the strongest, it broke
The oars on the land.

Instantly
A chill wind folded the bodies
In shrouds of the open sea
Instantly
The rose petals of the western sun
Strewed the hull of the upturned boat

Time rattled the keys of the elements
People chattered the universe was expanding
Newsprint rolled masses were invading
Of fresh, cold air

Ring

You had what you wanted
Water from the spring, star in the sky
A son in the cradle, fire in the hearth
A god in the temple, justice in the law
You had light in your eyes, hope in your words

You went where you wanted
Through helicon days and harvest nights
Along pale blue and darkening cliffs
You walked through a multi-coloured world
Of shores and mountains

Now you're alone
With nothing but the kiss of dust
They've ripped you inside out
A dribble of blood at the corners of your mouth
A swarm of flies round your dark head
Silent, spat upon, ignored
As if you weren't you
As if you'd never existed
In this world

Letter to a Friend

Mind what you say
Choose your words carefully
The rest is easily taken care of
It's the night I'm talking about
It doesn't make distinctions
Its guards are awake

You've a beautiful head
It holds innocent thoughts
And vigilant guards might easily detect them
I'm talking about the axes they're sharpening
For beautiful heads filled with innocent thought

Don't ask me where and how
The night in which I write to you
Mislaid all reason

Time has moved on
Midnight approaches
Black axes are being oiled for the white world
The night opens all roads to them
That's all
I wanted to tell you
Beautiful, wakeful head
Don't be angry my letters are so short
I'm tired, friend

Like a DOG

Land

Her secret, frankly, you will not guess,
Though she may hold your image in her memory.
From her maps, you will not find your way.
In her contours, you will not find your being.

In dreams, in life, her essence touched me.
I thought I could enclose the candle of her light.
And what I now see both is and is not her.
With my gaze, I paint afresh everything she is.

The riddle of her being is my solution.
I hide and wait for the ferocity of her embrace.
Crouched in grass with ants and grains of sand,
I hear the mean, bitter, mortal words that mark my transformation.

Is she the one? Or has she pushed me aside?
Restless, she will not even let her dead alone.
Here, where I am – and there where silence awaits me –
I seize and devour her like a hard crust of bread.

From her health, my sickness has its origin.
With her own seed in mind, she spits on death.
Though she turn to water, no other land could be mine.
Though all the falling blows, fate clears me a path.

The World We Changed

The late forms and the rose bud between two speakers
The weighed time the form of life in water the form of death in fire
Everything close everything distant at the same time
The places of childhood filled with the humming of a potter's wheel
Lumps of potter's earth clearly predicting chaos a wager
The potter's hands filthy and fertile plunged in the clay of events
Fire that clarifies choice the form of a jug the hardness of hearts
A world illuminated by thirsty mouths and wakeful drinking-fountains
The balance of luck and fulfilment a jug in a child's hand, merely
Pain revealed to the world as a game for the senses

You took from those places
The dead god the smashed temple the corpses of believers
The world was weighed in the desert that grew round you
The same world for everyone in the buzz of the forest in the blade
                                                              of a knife
The prophets of time played carelessly with fire and water together
The gold of the dead the baggage of the living grew wealthy by a
                                                        bloodied doorpost

IVAN KORDIĆ

Translations by DAVID CONSTANTINE / ANTONELA GLAVINIĆ

Ivan Kordić was born in 1945 in Bliznaci, near Mostar, and studied Croatian literature at the Teachers College in Dubrovnik, Croatia. He edited the literary journals *Zivot* (Life) and *Lica* (Faces), and is currently an editor at BiH Radio and Television. Strongly influenced by the lyrical tradition of earlier Herzegovinian poets, he is a poet of both the elemental and the metaphysical, with death a predominant motif. Well-known for his television commentaries during the war, he remained in Sarajevo throughout the siege.

Main publications: *Ruddy* (1964), *A Roar on the Sun's Battlefield* (1967), *The Fugitive Veil* (1972), *A House under the Sky* (1977), *Evening Wine* (1980), *A Verandah Overlooking the Sea* (1984), *Beyond Certain Years* (1985), *Poetry* (1987), *The Jerusalem Wall* (1990), *The Lie, the Hatred and the Crime* (essays, 1993), *We Searched for the House* (1993), *A Tomcat in Sarajevo* (1995) and *Like Stories, Like Poems* (1995).

House under the Sky

House under the sky
Or above the sky
Silence in the home
And a spider in the corner

Where is there anything that lives?
What still haunts?
Inside the old coat
Is that a heart beating?

The walls are naked, the roof
The meadows, woods and rivers are naked and alone
Does nothing touch you now?
Will you have no reunion now with anything?

Nothing fits. There is only
A tree under the sky.
My mother is dead
My brothers are old.

Open the Window, Mother

Open the window, mother
The men of blood are coming as wedding-guests

They will dig out the hearth

With fire they will abolish the shadows
From under our starlit tree

Neither shields nor prayers
Will serve us now
And the lovely spread of the ivy will perish with the door-post.

It Is the Wind Swaying You in Fits and Turns

Don't bow
Stand up to it
See there: a house, a tree, a hill
That will not easily be moved

It is the wind swaying you in fits and turns

Only you know you know you know
Why you are the one the wind wishes to move
When the tree, the hill, the house
Are standing still

Open your eyes but do not look

Wherever you look it will be wrong
The images are blowing about you in the wind
Nothing, nothing
Only the fits and starts of the the twisting wind.

Evening Wine

The voices in the evening are carriers of fear.
It is a smell
Sweetish
Our nostrils know, it is the frequency
Regret and dread come in on. Listen,
Smell, the glory of our speech
Has gone to dust
Fistfuls of it
Timing our lives away.

On the conscience of the voices of the evening
Is what they dare not say.
Look for it in the pupil of the eye
Or in the light in wine
Little fearful anima
Little flickering spectre
There in our wine
That kept us warm
Like a hearth, a meadow or a mother
Like a house and home, like a smile
It will go out

And the days will die and all the loves will die
Across our laps
And we shall hug them to our hearts
And starve
In perfect fear
For want of the virtue of the loves and days

Among the stones
That live for ever
Witnessing.

SEMEZDIN MEHMEDINOVIĆ

Translations by KATHLEEN JAMIE / ANTONELA GLAVINIĆ *(poems),*
AMMIEL ALCALAY *and* IVANA DJORDJEVIĆ *(prose poems)*

Semezdin Mehmedinović was born in 1960 in Kiseljak, near Tuzla, and took
a degree in comparative literature at Sarajevo University. He has worked as a
labourer, barman and secretary of the Translators Union, and was editor of the
journal *Lica* (Faces) and *Valter* in the late eighties, and *Dani* (Days) in the early
nineties. With its urban inflection and focus on everyday life, his early work
(along with that of Ranko Sladojević) marked an influential turning-point in
contemporary Bosnian poetry. He wrote and directed (with Benjamin Filipović)
the film *Mizaldo or the End of Theatre* screened at the Berlin Film Festival in
1994. He edited a remarkable wartime magazine, *Fantom Slobode* (Phantom
of Liberty), and was chosen to represent Bosnian writers at the 1994 Frankfurt
Book Fair. He left Sarajevo in the autumn of 1995, and now lives in Virginia,
near Washington DC, where he works for Voice of America. See pages 82-87
for his essay *A Small Map of the World.*

Main publications: *Modrac* (1984), *Emigrants* (1990) and *Sarajevo Blues* (1995).

A Sudden Shift

I spent last night in a trench
with yellow rain salamanders;

today, slipped into a bath
full of warm scented foam.

They take a bit of getting used to,
these sudden shifts.

How much more simple, and a pleasure
when I write, and arrange

with just a sentence, a meeting
between Bernard Henri Lévy

and some moustached Bosnian politico
who says 'Brodsky? He's a proven anti-communist!'

[1988]

Zenica Blues

Its snowing today, for the first time this year;
and a yellow pick-up's overturned
outside the library:
heaps of multi-coloured pills
spilled on the asphalt.

Dusk gathers on the boulevard,
like the darkness in the bags beneath your eyes.
This snow will cover miles
of rusty steel.

Across the river, rugby players
in their black and red shirts
roll their own breath before them.
A youth with a video, head bowed,
records the damp tar-mac
in front of him. Nothing but that.
You pass by, trudging lovelessly.

Strange, but you haven't seen a fly
for a year – not even
in that hot summer.
Neither are there fish in the river,
only seagulls, lots – flying down
on completely sodden loaves.

From this spot, for example,
you couldn't see the city cemetery
till yesterday. Now, at the hill-top –
two graves, two brown cat's-paws
on the prison wall.

And things are becoming slowly clear:
you covered the light-bulb's
over-strong glare
with a sheet of yesterday's paper.

Now you lie, reading the headlines in gloom.
You're tired
of the long wait.

At last, brakes squeal by the window;
the car's lit up inside,
miniature red boxing-gloves
swinging from its rear-view.

A long exit from the city:
the driver wears his glasses
to tear tickets, now he's driving without them.
The convict's chatting pleasantly with the policeman.
Through a narrow street, and past a skip
with COMMUNITY CENTRE written on it
you emerge in the square.
And while you watch, your amazement
quite disappears:
an old man on the pavement
trips over a pigeon.

Slowly you're crossing the bridge.
That woman, her face red with excema
crams two little fists
into a string bag stuffed with apples.
She twists her neck to watch
the rows of buildings, blue, in fog –
so sad-looking, you think:
she's never coming back, to this city.

On the hill above Rajlovac
there are thousands of crows,
thick on the dry grass
and bare acacia trees.
They're moving toward the sun.
But tonight – January of the ninetieth year –
they just don't feel like it any more,
they stay still, with no desire
to quit Yugoslavia,
to flit, once and for all.

In the BALKAN café, the local poet's holding forth:
That's not history, what they put in schoolbooks –
history's in the archive of Zenica prison.
Last time I was here I saw that famous emigrant,
him they write a lot about now, and what a satrap!
A gentleman! But with so much gold who wouldn't be?
He used to sit here, drinking bitter coffee.
Now I'm here, and him – he's on a wicker chair
at a Swiss Lake, stroking his cat, just
hiccuping with all the mentioning he gets.
And he had two horrible dogs.
Were they Great Danes or Dobermanns? No matter.
Maws this dark, but they wouldn't kill you, no –
they just smell the piss of any would-be attacker;
and run to their master with his prick in their jaws.
Their master, whose suffering
the whole world drones on about, now.

Two kilometres out of Zenica
the bus enters a sharp bend:
You feel the weight of the girl
sitting beside you, her warm shoulder.
And you see: three bouquets of roses
in cellophane, Sellotaped to the cold cement.
Look, you say, just to get talking;
it won't hold much longer.
And she nods her head. As if she knows.

You look out of the bus:
someone's set light to the scrub:
the colour of fire against the grey-brown.
And running around are kids
with long sticks, supervising the flames.

Icy morning at the stop.
Still hot off the press, the paper
under your jumper keeps you warm;
but colder yet for watching those two
saying farewell with quick kisses.
Chilled to the bone and warm in embrace,
their specs collide.

The woman sitting next to you
talks to herself
All right – she says – *all right*
just without touching.
– All eyes turn toward you
you turn as well,
looking for the culprit.
Embarrassed, you look back
biting your shoulder.

And on the way home
you nip into a suburban café.
Fishermen crowd together at the bar.
Although you're here for the first time –
weird – it's like you've seen it before:
the fishermen in green waders,
and the giant bottles of Mataxa on the bar,
so big you could embrace them easily.
Maybe you yourself are someone else,
someone unknown to you.
Dwell on it, and that thought
would destroy you utterly.

A Sarajevo rocker, a Jew, and you
in the café's khazi –
when they take a leak together
men bond perfectly.

That's the way it is, says the Jew
and you nod your head in agreement
but of course it's not the way it is.
Nothing is certain
except the two circumcised men
over the chasm of the toilet bowl.

Without you, everything in this city
will be just the same. Oh, console yourself
– maybe a little different.
Like when you light a cigarette
with the giant gas-taper.
That's why you should remember some details:
for example, the jangle of the silver wedding band
against the window, or your glass;
and all the images that inevitably
surround your DISCOMFORT.
The clash of teeth in a kiss, for example,
before you recognise
the ghostly clank of bones
in the silence, which, perhaps
you invented
– just like the fear
of dying in winter
when clothes freeze on the line
and the vest's stiff ribs hang creaking.

Numinous

Come evening, we wait for the moment
when shapes open.
The sky is still dark
because of the shine of earthly things.
Then the buildings turn to cardboard;
black, flat, shadowed. Then the sky glows
and the Moon takes its brilliance in the middle of the war.

In that moment, the divine smile
of the elements' unthreatening power
illuminates everything,
including my wee boy, standing at the window with binoculars.

The Only Dream

The bicycle's upturned. Father
hooking back the chain, keeps his head bowed.
Many people are hanging about the garden.

– Dad, are these the dead?
Don't be scared, son,
you can play with them.

Under my foot, ants hide, bigger than brambles
and the swing, with no one on,
swoops toward the sky, then falls back.

They're wearing yellow macs, and looking
for a way out of the garden.
They glance at me, over their shoulders.

Then one of them approaches the wall,
takes in his hand a door-knob
where there isn't one, there's no door there.

But twenty years ago,
father, remember,
how there used to be?

The Stranger

One day, I too will set off alone
into the darkness of a grave
on Alifakovak, or some other
city hill, here
where I once knew everyone.
Now, I recognise no one at all,
except two or three –
and only at night, alone
from the past, do I look out
at the darkness of the city
from someone else's flat,
I, the stranger, the stranger.

An Essay

This evening stroll deserves a poem:
the aeroplane's wink above the suburbs
as it sinks toward a blueish dark;
the sparking wires above the trolleybus.
A woman has lost an earring on the street,
and as she turns back now to look for it
I suddenly feel pity: for her,
for the boy squinting at his reflection
in his bicycle-bell;
for the old man on the bridge, who whispers
*the river is run dry. How can this happen
here, of all places, where we're so humane?*
Even, in the end, a sorrow
for the scattering of freckles on my mother's face
as we walk along, with her trying to convince me
that where I think of him
or imagine him to be, there God exists.

Dates

On 17th January 1994, he was killed.
For every day since,
he's been dead.

He is dead today too –
Friday the 24th February 1995.
And every evening

something uncanny
happens to me.
When I step into the bathroom

I notice in the mirror
how over my left shoulder
a shadow grows.

It's not mine. And if I look back
over that shoulder,
what do I see?

A dream, but my eyes are open:
a raven has flown down to my table
and it speaks,

saying: *on the 17th May,
cherries will be ripe in Sarajevo.*

I hear it, and I wait.

[KJ]

Sarajevo Blues
a sequence from the book of the same title

Photographers

1) December, the year 1991. Sitting around in the Theatre Club, photographs by Mladen Pikulić on the wall (the show is called *Vukovar today...and tomorrow?*). The music is too loud; the guys and gals sit silently at their tables, pupils dilated. Overhead, waiters make their way through paths blocked by the dazed young bodies, huge stainless steel pitchers of draft beer and Coca-Cola in their outstretched palms. Bloody syringes lie on the floor in the toilet. And then, a young guy at one of the tables points to another young guy – the one in the picture crying before the background of Vukovar decimated by grenades – and says, in amazement: 'He's got the same sweater on I got.'

2) The photographers of Sarajevo – as opposed to their colleagues who come from abroad to collect their fees from dailies, weeklies and art magazines by trading in death – are the only chroniclers of war in this city; they run out of film and supplies and get no compensation for their work. This doesn't make them any different or their job more distinguished that that of surgeons, for instance, or firefighters. But their engagement is marked by an *intellectual morality*, something so rare in our parts both before and during the war. So a photographer made it possible for a junkie in a bar in Sarajevo to recognise his sweater on a guy in a picture from Vukovar. The shells hadn't started falling here yet, but you could see – and how – that Sarajevo had already started wearing Vukovar's sweater. Of this, the intellectuals – or at least those referred to as such – kept quiet.

The war didn't change anything; what, for instance, did writers do after the Library burned down? What about scholars and historians? Nothing. Maybe because they'd already stopped going there. But when the Writer's Union, when their café was lost, they wrote endless protests and polemics in *Oslobodjenje*. The destroyed Library appeared on thousands of photographs... It became, among other things, part of the professional pathos: the Library in the foreground as a standard postcard of Sarajevo (chosen by photographers).

Maybe the guy in the picture wasn't even alive any longer during Pikulić's 'Eyewitness of War' exhibit. Today, I don't even know if the guy who pointed to the sweater in the picture is still alive either. The title of the exhibit extended itself to the question: *and tomorrow?*

Everyone knew the answer to that was already contained in the question, but they hoped tomorrow wouldn't come.

I said everyone, but I am thinking first of the intellectuals who kept quiet, hiding in the promiscuous Sarajevo night, evading the moral obligation to at least say that levelling cities by shell wasn't right. A photographer was one of the few who found himself among those who asked questions.

After ten months of war, you can still find 'intellectuals' in Sarajevo asking: 'Why is this happening to us, and why so brutally?' Fools, they don't see that the answer is: Because!

Just because.

And that's why it's too late now for any questions.

The Imam of the Bey's Mosque

1) A girl opens the door to his house for me and I see him unexpectedly – his hands busy around the stove – in a light green sweater, smiling. The movement of his hand beckons me to sit. I look at the rows of videos by the television; my first thought, curiously, is: could there, among all these tapes, possible be a film by Yilmaz Guney? And that very instant, I give up asking him.

2) Efendi Spahić, the Imam of the Bey's Mosque, had three children and a grandchild killed by the shells that fell on Dairam. Before that, his wife too; as if God had taken her to Him, to protect her. So she wouldn't see. Here's what I think: there are neither major nor minor tragedies. Tragedies exist; only some can be described. Also, there are others for which any heart is too small. Those cannot fit in the heart.

3) I first saw this man on television: I trembled at the abundance of spiritual power by which he gathered sorrow into himself; he seems younger to me now, as he nears the table, putting down a pack of cigarettes, holding an ashtray, offering me one and saying: 'I liked tobacco once, then I stopped, and now I don't smoke any more.' He speaks softly. When I speak softly, my voice becomes hoarse because of the cigarettes. I stare at him attentively, searching for a sign to reveal the power that distinguishes him. We speak; he says: 'People can be divided into the stronger and the weaker, but you can't chastise the weak. There are reasons to justify their weakness: physical constitution, for instance. And a lot of other reasons. I could never slaughter a sacrificial lamb, a *kurban,* with my own hands, nor would

I ever have the strength to do such a thing. So be it.' Pointing out his own weakness, he shattered my naive conviction that signs of his strength could be seized at a glance.

4) We speak; he doesn't improvise. His answers to the questions I pose have been thought out in advance. It seems that, in his solitude, he has thought through everything. That's why you feel a lightness as he speaks, his clasped fingers hugging his knees. His thinking is literary, visual. His answers are complete so that, gradually, the conversation unveils a small lexicon of the Imam's solitude.

Army. The Sarajevan soldiers are hunters, or so the story goes: like hunters, they go about their business all week and then, on Saturday, go into the woods and kill a rabbit before heading back home. That's how the soldiers are, or so the story goes. They sit in cafés and then hop into their fancy cars and head for the top of Bistrik, by Mt Trebević, to shoot.

Bosnian Muslim. I think of Tolstoy. He writes of Hadji Murad – awestruck by his rugged strength – and says: He's like grass in the fall, the hay carts pass over it, but when the wheels move on, every blade rights itself again. That's how the Bosnian Muslims are: blades of fall grass.

Mudjihadeen. The West has no idea what this means. In translation, it means 'fighter'. For them, he's a terrorist who throws bombs in Paris cafés. But he fights to fulfil divine justice; for him, killing in revenge is a capital sin. The West can't see this from its apathetic heart.

Islam. Faith in expansion, but without imposition; it has no missionaries. An *I* that doesn't pronounce itself, while leaving its abundant, human traces everywhere. And that is the trait of great people.

5) I'm drawn to his measured way of speaking. All the questions I put to myself about this man have been betrayed. I call this, for myself and for lack of a better term, divine tolerance. As we pause – while Efendi Spahić gets up, pulls the door of the oven open and turns back with two pears on a tray – I take a look at the prints on the wall, one coppertint, all with motifs from Sarajevo's Old City. This is where I saw it, so that's why I'm appending it to the lexicon of our conversation here.

The Spirit of Sarajevo. Those Bosnian cafés come to mind: on the walls, the inevitable pictures with the same motifs: an old man with a fez holding a findjan; merchants gathered around a public fountain. There (in those cafés), pensioners in black berets with white packs of Drina cigarettes used to come by from their shops or from Friday prayers, and junkies used to come by, because of the cheap Coca-Cola. Sarajevo's tolerance, usually associated with the equilibrium of worshippers holding different faiths in the same narrow streets, just pronounces the naivete of historians. This is truly tolerance, and no one has written even one word about it: the equilibrium of Bosnian motifs in a picture on the wall with Coca-Cola; the same water boiling coffee for the old man in the beret and the longhairs in jeans shooting up in the shadow of a minaret. This wasn't of importance to anyone. Historians haven't, for example, written anything about the Old City's tradition of naive art. I peel the pear: the conversation moves on to a more serene level: I distinguish yet another concept, and enter it into the lexicon.

Emir Kusturica. He is like a cow who has given a lot of milk and then, banging his foot into the pail, knocks it down and spills everything, says Efendi Spahić. When we part, I go out into the street calmer than when I had come. As Efendi Spahić spoke of his misfortune, his eyes – as if from cold – narrowed gently. Nothing more. I went out with the scent of fall pears in my nostrils.

6) It's sunny, and the city is still enveloped in fog. Right at the bottom of the long, elegant steps to the Municipal Museum, Bokun sits: with his hair wrapped in a pony-tail, dark glasses and a black leather jacket, he looks like Michael Douglas's resigned double. Saturday: the weekend Chetniks are up on the hills: I tell him it's time we got off the street, but he waves his hand: 'This is my last cigarette. It wants the respect it deserves. And I can only give it that on the street. It's only here that I'm alone enough,' he says.

7) I try to compare Bokun's solitude with the solitude of Efendi Spahić. I run out of breath walking uphill.

Reader, if you go up Abdullah Kaukji street another 50 metres, when you turn around you'll see Sarajevo in fog, a world of sorrow; above it, you can see the rooftops of the Old City and, still higher, the minaret of the Bey's Mosque, isolated from the terrestrial, quotidian fog.

[AMMIEL ALCALAY *translations*: 169-172]

The Corpse

On the bridge we slowed down,
and watched dogs in the snow along Miljačka
tearing apart a human corpse.
Then we went on.

Nothing in me changed.
I listened to the snow spattering under tyres
like when teeth crush an apple;
and felt this wild desire

to laugh at you
because you call this place 'hell'
and run away; telling yourself
that outwith Sarajevo, death is unknown.

[KJ]

Death by Freezing

When Sarajevo lies covered with snow, when pine trees are cracked
by frost, bones in the earth will feel warmer than us. People will
freeze to death: a fireless winter approaches, a sunless summer is past.
The nights are already cold and, when somebody's pet dog barks from
a balcony, a chorus of strays barks back, in tones as sorrowful as a
crying child's. Only in this city does an Irish setter – normally an un-
usually cheerful dog – howl dismally in the night like Rutger Hauer
in the final scenes of *Blade Runner*. Snow will bury the city as war
has buried time. What day is it today? When is Saturday? I don't know.
The daily and annual rituals are dead. Who will print calendars for
1993 in December? There is day, there is night; within them there is
a man whose existence is defined by the end of the world. He knows
that the fullness would be diminished were it not for the looming
global catastrophe. Therefore he strikes a light at dusk: a wick
threaded through a metal ballpoint refill, affixed to a piece of cork
wrapped in tin foil, so that it floats on the surface of the cooking oil
which burns in a lamp made of an empty beer can: The cheerful
flame allows him to see that objects and the faces of dear ones have
an earthly glow; and that there is no plight but the failing of light.

Living Together

In *The Killing of Christ,* Wilhelm Reich says that there are souls who 'find spiritual fulfilment in devising evil', Hrvoje B. tells me. 'Such were those who crucified Christ, because they simply could not tolerate a soul aspiring to a universe of love. Nero, Caligula, Genghis Khan, Stalin – they could not bear the existence of souls like Bruno's, Gandhi's, or Lincoln's. For centuries, Bosnia has demonstrated that people of different nationalities and creeds can live in peace and love – that in itself is enough to make it an outrage. Therefore it is crucified, just like Christ before it.'

Fires

Having finished photographing the Vijećnica in flames, Kemo Hadžić was wounded by a shell fragment on his way home. It is hard to avoid mysticism in a war: My first thought was: his wounding is a warning. Kemo says he felt no pain as long as he was in shock. To feel pain, one must be conscious of pain. Whereas a state of shock, as long as it lasts, is a kind of stay in the beyond. It is also a plunge into the world of one's own art: what else, indeed, was this photographer doing, walking round the burning library, looking for the ideal angle and good lighting, capturing the waters of the Miljačka in his wide-angle lens. What was this but an artist's passionate desire to wrench its savage beauty from the horrid scene of death, to approach it from beyond. The artist's need to step into the unknown is fraught with risks, but it is on such a step that the power of art rests. Perhaps, I say, the shell fragments were a punishment for this heretical step? But perhaps I am just being esoteric, prompted by wartime anxieties, so that in a boy – whom Kemo, in shock, follows to the hospital and only notices after the doctor has seen to him, as he fans his sweating face with a folded newspaper – I recognise a being who does not belong to this reality. Because of that angelic gesture.

Shelter

I dart across the road to avoid a sniper bullet from the hill and run to meet the news photographers; secure in their shelter, they go about their work. Should a bullet hit me, they would take photographs so much more attractive than my life that – at that moment

– I am no longer sure whom I should hate more: the Chetnik with the sniper-lens or these apes with their Nikons. To the former I am a target pure and simple, whereas the latter confirm my utter powerlessness and intend to profit from it too. For all of them now in Sarajevo, death is a job to do. Life has shrunk and reduced itself to gestures. How touchingly comic is the gesture of a man who covers his head with a newspaper before running across the same road, fearful of sniper bullets. Bernard Henri Lévy has described the war in Sarajevo as a typical medieval siege. Yes, but present-day means of destruction are so much more devastating, which means that in this town you have no shelter; every second you are in peril of death. The feeling of powerlessness comes from the occupation of the space of my mortality by my own body, and mortality, due to constant shelling, is the most frequent thought here. Mental survival requires as comforting a shelter as can be found. Experience has shown that the most efficient shelter is made of books. In our part of town a shell hit the gas main and by morning the disgusting smell of hissing gas had saturated the street. Experts said this was very dangerous, and the next day we used books to bar all access to gas. There were plenty of books there, as the nuclear shelter that had served as library storage in peacetime had been emptied. When a shell falls, the books act as a net to collect the fragments. An acquaintance of mine owes his life to the fact that his wife used to work in the Marxist library, where she could have free copies of Lenins, Engelses and Kardeljs. That books save lives is a typical Kafkaesque metaphor turned reality for us. A poet in Sarajevo built a bunker out of books; on the front window, as a sentinel observing the front line, stands a thick book with an expensive-looking glossy dust jacket: *To Victory with Tito*. What an unusual choice of book to serve as inscription and protect the poet's home. I have an inscription myself: a friend has given me a stylised drawing of a sword and a rifle framed by something written in Arabic script, copied on a fax machine. True, I used to think that an inscription had to be written by hand, and that it was as living writing that it had the power to protect. This way a fax machine mediates between me and God, and I believe myself safe.

Karadžić

After Radovan Karadžić had informed the world public of the existence of Muslim camps where Serbs were maltreated, TV cameras easily confuted his fictitious list. Pictures showed unambiguously that the Koševo stadium was no concentration camp: untended grass grown wild, and stands devastated by shell craters. Radovan's intentions had not been to deceive the world public: he knows it is quick to discern a lie. Being a liar does not bother him, nor does he care what the whole wide world will think of him. The important thing for him is to convince his compatriots. The Bosnian Muslims may have forgotten the genocide whose object they have been; not so the Chetniks. They believe they will go unpunished, as they have so many times already.

A boy told me an interesting story about how Chetniks multiply like gremlins in contact with slivovitz; they do, and they go slaughtering Muslims, because that is not forbidden and no punishment awaits them.

The world sees what they are doing, but this does not mean it will thrash them for it. The world has known this before, without ever touching a hair in their beards. And so Karadžić sends foreign reporters to film empty football stadiums while he plunders on and butchers on under cover of darkness. He is a Chetnik awoken after fifty years of hibernation – recent technological developments amaze him. His political marketing is reduced to 'You can take my word for it.' Thus, when he realised how miraculous television and publicity were, he was pleased. He liked to be broadcast live; pandering to his vanity, he lied and fudged to YUTEL viewers. He went further still: when his heroes shooting at babies are filmed by foreign reporters he makes a live appearance on *Sky News* to deny the 'erroneous' reports. The picture of the empty stadium at Koševo is a touching refutation of all his statements. A tall-stalked sunflower at the edge of the track proves that no Serbs are imprisoned at the stadium; it proves both that no one has been there for months and that human bodies did once fill up the stands. It was sown by a man who munched on sunflower seeds to soothe his football fan's neurosis; he dropped one or threw it away in disgust, and the seed grew into a plant in the playing field. It is Radovan's sunflower; he could not have sprung up without it. The sunflower is a living icon of a time that can never be restored.

Bernard Henri Lévy

In front of television cameras, talking to a reporter, Bernard Henri Lévy is forced to duck and seek shelter, while bullets buzz all around him. Sitting on the ground, he goes on talking. In Sarajevo, Lévy speaks of what is going on in Sarajevo. Pictures of this will circle the globe; he has seen it all, there is no deception, he knows what is going on here – his words are addressed to Europe. If the decision were his, the city would be free by morning. He was among the first to open the eyes of his nation – blind to the evil of concentration camps – to all the horrors of the Gulag. To take a stand on concentration camps has been the duty of the twentieth-century intellectual. Such a committed intellectual was celebrated in his *Praise*..., a fine and instructive book. Before the camera, not without elation, he talks while bullets whizz all around him. He shows a thinker's perverse pleasure in having his views confirmed at the very moment when he is announcing them to the world. Lévy's commitment thus becomes an instrument of television; he is a participant in this war, everybody sees that now. The grand narcissism of a thinker who will, in fact, say nothing to a world blind to the truth, but his figure and words will help the mass-media monster turn war into a war game.

Massacre

Pictures of the large-scale massacre in the Ferhadija mosque. Pictures of the dead and butchered have turned into advertisements for war. Who cares that these people have names: they are no more than images. Television has translated them into its own cold language. The camera empties an image of its psychological content and turns it into information. All the ensuing massacres were merely the same image multiplied. The world, therefore, sees what is going on here. Does anyone in the whole wide world grieve with us? No one. Because television knows what human nature is really like, that there is no compassion in it as long as tragedy does not touch us personally. The sense of tragedy arrived with the coffins draped in the American flag, not before. Not through television reports from Vietnam. We are experiencing massacres; we grieve for our own tragedy. That is all. Perhaps we could derive meagre consolation from the fact that we are more aware of the nature of the media. We see through it as we see the inside of a computer drawing of a car, undistracted by the purplish glow of the monitor screen. The rest is scenery: a CNN cameraman, unreal in his novelty and completeness, looks down a blind alley in ruins at Bistrik. There is no one in the deserted street, just flames emerging from the door of a burning store.

Chetnik Positions

First the excavator arrived: It dug trenches in the ground, and a lorry brought concrete slabs to line them with. Tanks were dug in at the sides, so that only their cannon protruded. Guns as well. Our rifles cannot reach them. Perhaps they could spend the winter in such trenches? It is August now; they get tobacco from Niš, brandy from Prokuplje. I don't know where their women come from, but I have seen them through binoculars. One of them has placed an inflatable mattress by the trench and is sunbathing in a swimsuit. She lies there for hours. Then she gets up, goes to the cannon, pulls the cord and fires a shell on the town at random. She listens briefly for the explosion and watches for its source. She even stands on tiptoe, innocently. Then she goes back, coats her body with suntan lotion, and surrenders herself to serenity.

Glass

I go to the window and look at the cracked glass panels of the 'Jugobanka' building. I could stand there for hours. A blue glass facade. One floor above the window from which I watch, a professor of aesthetics is out on his balcony: he adjusts his glasses and combs his beard with his fingers. I see him reflected in the blue facade of 'Jugobanka', in the cracked glass panels which turn the scene into a living cubist painting on a sunny day.

[IVANA DJORDJEVIĆ *translations*: 173-178]

Hero

He's a hero, says the soldier in fatigues, pointing at the kid kneeling on the parquet floor. Killed a Chetnik, he says. The boy put the ammunition belt and the old M48 down on the floor: he smiles, completely carried away, as he plays with plastic cars and makes the sounds of an engine. On Vraca, he says, after agreeing to tell the story, my friends took some shots with a Kalashnikov and nothing. Then I let go twice and the Chetnik just rolled over. My rifle kills at five kilometres, he said, scratching his forehead with a toy car.

Milomir Kovačević

Ever since he's been a photographer, he's worn the same kind of iffy reddish-green sweater. He wore it in peace and Milomir Kovačević shot the entire war in Sarajevo in it. He managed to be wherever something was happening because it all came under eye, even the body, for which one sweater is enough. Ambitious photographers are trying to show Sarajevo in ruins, as a place of death. From their pictures of the charred UNIS skyscraper, you can't see the former beauty of the city in the valley: students in shirtsleeves stroll by the university on a sunny day as snow on the peak of Mt Trebević reflects off the blue glass facade of the high-rise. Because the gaze has been so violently disrupted in this city, such photographs are descriptive, of no artistic merit. A photograph by Milomir Kovačević: with legs crossed – a boy? a girl? I'm not sure – a naked creature on the pavement sits in the lotus position. Nothing in the picture points to the war: the beatific smile and wire-rim glasses only make the similarity between this androgynous figure and Ghandi more apparent. Separated from the surrounding war, it would still be an interesting shot, a 'moment of the world's totality' (P.D. Ouspensky). Yet, it is a war photograph that, paradoxically, is more accurate than those revealing the devastation of Marindvor. Everyone in Sarajevo, accustomed to death, lives through so many transcendental experiences that they have already become initiates of some deviant form of Buddhism. If the aggression lasts another month or so, many of them will believe that a chestnut falling on Wilson's Promenade carries more weight than a grenade.

Shell

Shells are constructed so shrapnel can't be cleaned out of the flesh, that's why there are so many amputations. Their power is a great stimulant to the soldier, that corpse in a trenchcoat, to his military autism. The utmost proclamation of existence is a soldier's signature on the casing of a shell. Europe and its 'western sin' makes the end of the world imaginable, that need to affirm her own existence is also her curse. Graffiti scratched into bathroom walls: *this is my name, I exist*; and the shells that levelled Sarajevo's maternity ward signed in oil: *this is me and by my being I will destroy other lives*. That's Europe, a sign of weakness: endless self-affirmation, the end of the world. Shells killing kids. Imaginations turned 180 degrees, gone wild, emptied of memory. This is probably sheer esoterica: I think about how their blocked consciousness is not a reaction to the images of war, but nature preparing them for long years of battle. What kind of curriculum will be put in place for kids ripped apart by shrapnel as sharp as razors? Imagine a teacher assigning 'Snail House' or 'The Enchanted Saddle'... It's easier to think of war as their only school. And there are plenty of shells, they're so devastating that only the Schwartzeneggers have a chance to survive – at least according to postmodern theorists – left to themselves, wandering naked through the global desert and the infosphere, new nomads freed from feudal prejudice, not as members of a nation but as carriers of information they'll exchange between themselves together in the planetary community. Right now it's true that shells are falling on Bosnia, in Sarajevo, but it's unlikely that's where it will end.

Loss

I remember how – on my first reading – Goethe's *Der Erlkonig* really got to me: the part about the father holding the dying child in his arms. The magnitude of the child's fear and the father's powerlessness made my hair stand on end! I've thought of that poem so many times this past year, and not because the feelings it once evoked came back to me again and again in this reality permeated by the presence of death. Rather because death was so present that I couldn't identify it through specific tragedy. I invoked the feeling to induce my own sense of *the tragic.*

All in all, that was just a sham. The essence of poetry is that we experience the words of a poem as if informed within us, or as if we ourselves had uttered them. From this it becomes possible to identify with the tragic in Goethe's classical construction. It looks like the war controls our sorrow, holding it in reserve for those dear or close to us...

Very few people haven't had something happen to them. Everyone keeps their distance from those whose tragedies are *fresher.* That's why I feel uneasy writing about my own loss, but I write from pressure deep within.

My father died. Not here, he was in another city under siege, in Northern Bosnia. I love him as much as a son loves a father and I still haven't gotten used to the feeling that he's gone. I put off my encounter with his death and, now, when I think of him, the images that come to me are joyous and sad, innocent.

He hardly ever got sick. Once he had tonsilitis that got infected: I can see him contorting his eyeballs to have a full view of the mirror while I – following his directions – blow aluminium chloride over his swollen tonsils through a plastic straw. This is one of the first things that comes to mind and every time I remember, I smile. And this protects me from attacks of melancholy, it holds my balance. He was a miner, and he possessed a perfect sense of simplicity in showing his feelings. He couldn't be counted among the *strong*. He displayed his weakness so easily that I often felt the need to hug him. For instance, I started buying cigarettes quite early. As soon as I began, he started buying them too: he was like someone who thought he'd missed out on something and had to race to make up for it – like someone who measured out his own years according to the growth of his son.

I can't let myself think of him that way now because I'm afraid I'd just fall apart. The war created a dual selfishness in me: I'm shaken by a death that has taken place far from here, and I'm quenched by the death in this city that only fills me with a dull sense of dread. The other part of my selfishness has to do with delaying an encounter with my father's death. Like yesterday when I avoided telling him something that I knew I had to tell him so that, obstinately, it remains unsaid. And this that is *unsaid* gets to me, and that's why I call upon images of plain happiness.

With sharp pruning shears my father cuts the dry limbs in the warm April afternoon and sings *Hey, I'm cutting the pearly apple...*

Visit [1990]

He keeps ringing until I get up
And when he comes in he looks at the paper on the table.
No inspiration? My father asks.
Look – he says – the lake is so frozen
That heavy trucks can go over it
If they have chains on their winter tyres.
He keeps talking until I'm convinced the
World can be looked at from another perspective
And I see people walking across the lake
Each one with a fish-hook in their mouth.
           I ask myself
Which one of us will die first?
But only after he took off his jacket
To show the two bites of a clothespin
On the shoulders of his white shirt

[AMMIEL ALCALAY *translations*: 178-181]

NEW VOICES

Igor Klikovac was born in 1970 in Sarajevo, where he lived until 1993, when he came to England. He took a degree in comparative literature and librarianship at Sarajevo University. Parts of his first collection of poetry, *Last Days of Peking* – written on the move between Sarajevo, Zagreb and London – have appeared in translation in England, the Czech Republic, France and Slovenia. In 1995, with Ken Smith, he founded *Stone Soup*, a literary quarterly published in London in bilingual format (English and the languages of the former Yugoslavia). He now lives in London, where he works as a freelance writer.

Mirsad Sijarić was born in 1970 in Sarajevo and studied philosophy at Sarajevo University until the outbreak of the war. He was mobilised at the beginning of the attack on Bosnia and remained on duty throughout the war. He is presently completing a degree in History at the University. A number of his early poems appeared in *Phantom of Liberty*, a journal edited by Semezdin Mehmedinović; his first book, *Eagle*, was published in 1995.

Aneta Benac-Krstić was born in 1954 in Sarajevo and took a degree in journalism at Sarajevo University. She has published two collections of poetry, *A Fertile Jug* (1976) and *Black Sun* (1995). She continues to live in Sarajevo, where she works in the department of educational programming for Sarajevo TV.

Damir Ovčina was born in 1973 in Sarajevo and took a degree in South Slavonic literature at Sarajevo University. He has published a book of poems and short stories, *Autumn Days*, and continues to live in Sarajevo, where he teaches Bosnian literature and language.

Asmir Kujović was born in 1973 in Novi Pazar, Serbia, and has lived in Sarajevo since 1991. He was mobilised during the war and is currently completing a degree in philosophy at the University of Sarajevo. His first collection, *A Military Book of Dreams*, was published in 1997.

Mustafa Zvizdić was born in 1970 in Sarajevo. He was mobilised during the war and now studies Bosnian literature at Sarajevo University. His first collection, *Games with Wax*, was published in 1996.

Saša Skenderija was born in 1968 in Vitez. He took a degree in comparative literature and librarianship at Sarajevo University and did postgraduate studies in information science at the University of Prague. He has published two collections of poetry, *Drawing a Phoenix* (1990) and *It Ain't Like the Movies At All* (1993). He now works as an assistant lecturer at the Institute of Information Studies at Charles University, Prague, and as a systems librarian at the State Technical Library.

Fahrudin Zilkić was born in 1968 in Plav, Montenegro, and has lived in Sarajevo since 1981. He was mobilised during the war, now works as a journalist for *Oslobodjenje* and is completing a degree in philosophy at Sarajevo University. His first collection, *The Last People*, was published in 1995.

IGOR KLIKOVAC

Translations by IGOR KLIKOVAC / KEN SMITH

* * *

Getting ready for a trip. In a borrowed sports bag
you pile clothes upon books. Paltry things out of sight
you deliberately forget. You sing to yourself.
Unbidden haste – a Czech tourist's itching feet – spurs you on.

You'd like to go as far as possible, but zipping up the bag,
you feel you've already arrived somewhere.
Opened scissors on the table, small change in the lee side
of a pocket.

Outside, the mortars are thundering – as far as you are now,
you won't get.

Airborne Hazards

From the neighbouring balcony, a boy threw
planes folded from an illustrated magazine;
disappointed with the shortness of their flight, he was oblivious
of the siren's wail blending with a hollow flutter
left in the air by the paper's headlong plunge.

We are wrong to underestimate indecision.
Was it not the childlike absent-mindedness that,
like the hesitant touch of the old masters, completed the marquetry
on the faces of our killers – a metaphor for a sweet,
elegant ambush, a picture of a distracted butcher
pleasantly smiling, while with the unerring routine of an entertainer
he juggles the cellophane and bloodless guts.

Playback

In the glass across the road: two heads and a fragment
of torso – a girl sitting on a boy's lap, the sequence
blurred by driving rain and a tram's heating.
As if searching for a certain spot, she hesitates a while
before kissing the tip of his chin. Then
they laugh in profile, a brief contortion
into anonymous coats.

Stirring the ends of my toes in a thin gruel
of polyester and newsprint, I feel in the shoe
a warmth which almost evokes the intimacy
between us as I observe them: mouths open
filled with pale neon, clinging together
in the disconnected tremolo of their voices.
Caught up in the sudden grating of the passing trams
their laughter is as heavy
as the lead cast out with a fish-hook.

Festival of the Dead in a Second-Division Stadium

Workmen mark lines on a football pitch
for an important Sunday match.
The chalky dust carried by the wind surrounds them
and rises high above their heads like ash
at a September festival in Kyoto or Osaka.

The souls of the dead are taking the best seats.

MIRSAD SIJARIĆ
Translations by AMMIEL ALCALAY

TO DEFEND

I JOINED UP WITH THE RESISTANCE
IT WAS ABOUT TIME
THE BATTLES HAVE ALREADY BEEN GOING ON FOR A WHILE
AND EVEN THOUGH WE'VE ORGANISED A DEFENCE
THE ENEMY IS DEFINITELY ADVANCING
THE CITY'S SHRINKING THE OUTSKIRTS ALMOST GONE
THE WALLS OF OUR HOUSES ARE SOLID
THE NEWS REPORTS OUR SUCCESS
THE FIGHTER'S MORALE IS HIGH
BUT I DON'T EXACTLY FEEL SAFE HERE
I ASK MYSELF HOW LONG WE CAN HOLD OUT
THINGS ARE GETTING TOUGHER
BANDAGES ARE LOW
FOOD JUST ONCE A DAY
WE TAKE AMMO FROM THE DEAD
AND WHAT'LL HAPPEN WHEN THEY'RE NOT HERE ANY MORE...

TO LIE DOWN

I LIE DOWN BEHIND A TREE
ON THE GROUND IN THE GRASS
I SEE THE MOON THROUGH THE CLOUDS
THE OUTLINE OF HOUSES AND TREES
I SEE THE DARKNESS
EXCEPT FOR THE CRICKETS
THE SILENCE IS DULL
LOOKS LIKE THE ENEMY'S CALMING DOWN
BUT I COULD SWEAR I HEAR THEM
TWO OR THREE
I WAIT
TERRIFIED
ALONE
THEY MUST BE REAL CLOSE

TO CONTRIBUTE

ARMED LIKE WE'RE HUNTING FOX
OR LYING IN WAIT FOR A WIDE-EYED GROUSE
WE LAUGH AND OPEN FIRE
AT OUR UNSEEN ENEMIES
SO WE TOO CAN CONTRIBUTE TO THE GENERAL BREAKDOWN
AND INCOMPREHENSION OF THINGS

TO FORGET

IN MOMENTS OF CALM
AS I PASS THE SO-CALLED STREETS BY THE SO-CALLED BUILDINGS
OF OUR SO-CALLED CITY
THE SKELETONS OF CIVILISATION ARISE EVERYWHERE
FURNITURE CLOTHING PHOTOGRAPHS
MARRIAGE PHILOSOPHY
FORGOTTEN
TO EVERY QUESTION FIRE PROVIDES
A QUICK SIMPLIFIED ANSWER

TO KNOW

I DON'T KNOW
MY PHONE HASN'T RUNG FOR A LONG TIME
AND IT'S DARK IN THE HALLWAY
AFTER SUNSET
I DON'T OPEN THE DOOR FOR ANYONE
THE PEOPLE FROM THE NEXT APARTMENT
LEFT QUIETLY
AS IF THEY HADN'T LIVED LOUDLY
I NEVER LIGHT A FIRE AT NIGHT
I'M AFRAID THEY'LL NOTICE
AND I SIT AT MY TABLE LESS AND LESS AFTER DARK
IT'S TOO QUIET TO THINK OF FOOD
FROM TIME TO TIME I LISTEN TO THE RADIO THAT'S TRUE
BUT ALL I CAN
REALLY TUNE INTO IS FEAR

AND WHEN THEY SHELL US
I'M CALM
SINCE I KNOW
HE TURNS HIS BACK TO THEM
AND PRAYS FOR MY SOUL

TO BE READY

HE SAYS:
PUT YOUR COAT ON
GET THE LAUNDRY READY FOOD AND THE GOLD
DON'T TOUCH THE PAINTINGS
WE'LL ONLY TAKE WHAT WE NEED
I'LL BE AT THE DOOR
AND THE CIGARETTES ARE WITH ME
IF THEY BURST INTO THE BUILDING TONIGHT
PLEASE
BE QUIET AND BE READY
BE WITH ME

TO DISCUSS

WE'RE SITTING ON THE BALCONY IN THE DARK
DISCUSSING THE MEANING OF BEING AND ART IN PEACE
THE PROSAIC NATURE OF THESE PHENOMENA ANGERS AND STIRS US
THE ARHYTHMIC POEM OF WAR CAN BE HEARD LOUDER AND LOUDER
WE WITHDRAW INTO THE APARTMENT
CARRYING OUR CHAIRS WITH US
THE DISCUSSION CONTINUES
SOMEONE CRACKS A JOKE

ANETA BENAC-KRSTIĆ
Translations by FRANCIS R. JONES

A Shattered Honeycomb
(to the ruins of my grandparents' house in Plehan)

Keep me in your atmosphere Orion
I'm coming with a seashell of well-hemmed words
Words which bear drowsily quivering linden trees
whose coronets of blossoms in the breeze
draw the figures of my solitude
A long wall with my grandfather's beekeeping hat
carved as it were into the marble facing
My father's laughter preserved
pinkish blue in the corners of the room
swathes my arms like silken velvet

Keep me in your atmosphere Orion
I'm coming with a seashell of well-hemmed words
Words which bear the dense heavy folds of dark
from which eternity issues forth
and to which it returns
Ruins whose dust is the sole certainty
                              of what is to come
As your hour-glass sets great processions of nations
moving off into timelessness Orion
and these terrible times of death
the omnipresent

Invisible Statues

Solitude has the weight of wind which clings to the face
Of wind which scatters the prints of bodies left in the air
Which scatters someone's timid gesture
A smile and breath of delight
A clenched hand and a book enveloped with fingers
The lifted wrists of a running man

Hands lowered in acceptance and unwanting
Fear and dread laid on the Tomb of the Seven Brothers
from a thousand eyes

Solitude has the weight of wind which clings to the face
Of wind which scatters the prints of bodies left in the air
Which scatters someone's foot consumed by fire
An optic arc with the image, trapped and unrepeatable
of a passing city
A decapitated corpse
Someone's mangled arm-socket
Someone's body breaking into a run
Someone's broken body

Sarajevo Nocturne

A time is coming for slender birch trees to fall
like star pollen settling on drowned hills
from a quiet eternity
into vistas beyond our grasp

A solemn sky
bears silver rocking chairs with our jackets
folded in prayers for this city under siege
Winds are signposts for the dead
whose daily blood trickles from the corner of Dalmatinska Street
towards the river caught napping the cat-nap of death
Poplars rise in unfathomable clouds
their crowns forming
a final cry

A time is coming for slender birch trees to fall
like star pollen settling on drowned hills
from a quiet eternity
into vistas beyond our grasp

Threads

On only one
of the endless skein of slender threads
which you shape into
a colour, a word, a dream and a love
and then assemble into a sense
and a new world on white
do our lives depend

Sometimes you'll weave them into masts and sails
for a boat in which you take me out to the cape
for only up there can the whole
expanse and depth be seen

Today in the space of your eyes
I see a line of deaths
improvised from the things I touch in this room

DAMIR OVČINA
Translations by DAVID WHEATLEY / ANTONELA GLAVINIĆ

Skeletons and Us

from the beginning they're strangers
we cry hysterically
in childhood when they poke through the skin
every day we hide them away
most often forget all about them
insulated by skin and transparent fabrics
decades pass and we hardly remember them
we give ourselves to words
to traffic to football
while they wait their turn
stooping ever so slightly
always prepared for a change in the schedule
for sudden burial
and poignant removal from mass graves

Poem for My Cells

I have never been on intimate terms
with the masses of my cells
they are somewhere deep within me
I know that they're divided by walls
that they have cytoplasms
that they change
and are numberless
lessons are drawn on the blackboard
I keep my cells up
all night
immerse them in water
get them out of bed early
rather foolishly convinced of their loyalty
very rarely taking seriously the possibility
of their dividing the wrong way

Ad

The last cuffs of winter hurry along the passers-by
through the window, as if through a camera
I observe the early evening scenes
music in the room transforms this moment
into a TV ad
but outside nobody's aware of this
or the tune that's throwing us outside Time
that's transforming our figures
into black dots on manuscript paper

ASMIR KUJOVIĆ
Translations by FRANCIS R. JONES

Return from Guard Duty

A cigarette's walk away from the barracks
sweet-corn grows in rose gardens;
dead sober, we wheel on the spot
and stagger down the road to the tracks.

He feels his hand in plaster through
the pain, not through another's touch.
Nor does he notice the hand that places
a cup of hot coffee on the table.

Because the night is bright with explosions;
besides, he's still got mist on his specs,
and a leaf, out in the yard, under
the raindrops, is beating like a heart.

Trench No. 3

In a beat-up shed
in a car-wrecker's yard
a soldier's cleaning mud off his boots
with the end of a twig.
Another's carving a cigarette holder
and a miniature water-wheel for a stream
whose flow has been turned by the rain.
A third's drawing mosques and naked women
on the wall with a charred stick.

Lads absorbed in serious work
in a car-wrecker's yard,
and outside it's sunny –
the season of maggoty cherries.

MUSTAFA ZVIZDIĆ
Translations by ANTONELA GLAVINIĆ *and* JOHN HARTLEY WILLIAMS

Told by Mustafa of the Noble and Mad Zvizdić Family

I have no home, I have fear.
A suitcase I have, in the suitcase fear.
With the suitcase I travel.
I travel, I travel,
against the barren bars I press my face.
I don't look over my shoulder, no ticket inspector,
it's a free ride to futility.
History has its logic,
and I – paranoia.
Third on the left in the herd,
I smile before the execution.
The cold is a knife,
mercy is not what I beg.
This is all me:
the rustling of the coat,
the rippling of the tea.
This is all me:
the itching under the hat,
the mouth of nicotine breath.
Who's that smiling out of the mirror?
Since the death of your husband, madam,
your son's grades have dropped suddenly...
Mustafa is inarticulate,
he can't tell a joke...
Mustafa is a fraud,
his poetry is swarming with clichés...
Just like Santić, just like Santić,
my son is a true Herzegovinian...
You are gifted, Mustafa,
as gifted as Sidran...
Mustafa is a weakling,
Mustafa is a shadow of a man...
I slip through time
like a fish through palms.

I won't go drowning in café tables,
it's not that bad.
God loves men without hope.
They are the meekest.

[JHW/AG]

The Hump

I

There's no getting away from it

You avoid mirrors
Shop windows
You run away from your own shadow

You hate your profile
Caught in the reflection of someone else's spectacles

You hate your breath
Snaking downwards

That growth
Towards the ground

Those eyes
Without sky

Underneath boots
Amidst insects

II

A hump is a bow without an arrow
A bow is an arrow under the burden of years
No bad conscience there

The hump loves parks
And benches with backs

The shining past
Is what the arrow remembers

Truth has the shape of an iron bar
Folded by a winner

The bow is truth
With the arrow in a museum

The truth is a hump
The hump is a stump

From which the beaten hang

III

The hump isn't youth

Youth is frizzy hair
And a military posture

Youth is a soldier's song
Driven against a wall

Youth is our future
The future in a stampede

The hump is youth that's survived

[JHW]

Home

That home grew directly out of my stomach
Blossomed at all four corners of the world
With its gutters chimneys
Home in whose heart a table cloth glowed
The crimson work of my mother's
In moments of tenderness I'd say:
A lump of meek biography that defies the skies
But at times of morning stupor:
That grinning jaw keeps dragging
Through my troublesome dreams

The home of packet soup
The home of inert silver
The home of my cheap shaving kit
The home of my hands
Of my astigmatic gaze
The home that burnt up one spring day
The home in which disappeared
The hard impression of my thumb
My white mouth of silence
The white scream
Of my unfulfilled world

[AG/JHW]

SAŠA SKENDERIJA
Translations by FRANCIS R. JONES

Billie Holiday

Nitrates poisoned the tenuous soul
of my old love. Mija Z, jazz singer and first lady
of the Maribor Spring, from 7 to 3 a worker
in the local nitrate factory, loved my thin
body, bathed it that summer in cold
water from a broken boiler. On the photos that
remain, her figure is unreal, floating
on the sandalwood smoke of joss-sticks and gazing
at the big black-and-white poster of Billie Holiday,
as if acid has flowed over its contours.
Something similar has happened to her voice
on the cassettes, it's going hoarse. The dull spleen
of the double bass and the despair she bewitched me with,
mezzo-soprano husky with nitrate fumes.
In the autumn of our love, despairing at my
youth, my leaving, she swallowed some pills,
had an abortion… Loneliness. A bitch of an autumn,
melancholy.

Craftsmen
(for Susan Sontag)

Photography and death – killing, freezing
the instant – is too hackneyed an
analogy, nothing short of a cliché.
The sniper and the press photographer
at the Tito-Gorky Street crossroads
are making the same abstraction
of my fate, condensed to the ten metres
of street I have to sprint across.
The artist, the master craftsmen, are waiting,
my hesitation fills them with
professional angst, which works
in my favour, ups my chances.
And that's just it, the root of the problem:
murderers, like artists, tend to
over-dramatise, go for mutual
glorification, cheap effects.
Firing at nothing. Sniper and photographer.
The same cross-hairs centre their shots.

Untitled

Landscape chained in the lenses of your
sunglasses, thought given rhythm
by the even rattle of the speeding train, your
hand in my groin. This is a joy, sweetheart,
this is my love, the best that's left
of me. The outcome came out of the blue,
where we last expected it. I no longer
remember how, or why, just that you're here beside
me. Emerging too slowly, the scent of your skin,
factions of perception in the lenses of your
sunglasses. Travelling. How can we keep
our cool, sweetheart, how can we hold out?

FAHRUDIN ZILKIĆ
Translations by FRANCIS R. JONES

Ricochet

It's when you define the world's sides,
when you run across a section of road
between two bushes.

It's when you hear the shot,
and while you're lying flat on your
face you're spattered with gravel.

Ricochet –
it's when a year later
you recognise the scar on the stone
where your life went on again.

The Last Men

I

When we leave, oh God,
or when we return,
count us
just the same –

so the dead know that they've died.

II

Of everything
I've learnt
at this distance:
living a quiet life
and knowing
he won't always miss –
not even miss me

III

When I think of those who were hit
I absorb thoughts of friends:
Saja, blown to bits up on Igman.
Amir who lost his bottle –

in a mortar attack, in Moševićka,
he stood up yelling: 'Go on, shoot me, you motherfucker!'
And they shot him.
By half a fingernail.
His heart was cut in two –

one half death
and one half the life of those who remember him.

IV

Between the shells and the death
there are pauses,
enough to freeze you to the bone.
Pauses
like whistles,
like choices:
who in a few days
will emerge less worried
and be just grass?

V

Hands can't picture
what the soul senses.
Between them and me
there's just a yawning silence.

In it I scribble,
scribble, scribble…

VI

Shadows are spying on me.
I show them who I am, and go
so close
that I become one of them.

When I want to escape,
it's late,
I can't find the way –
just footprints,
footprints, footprints…

VII

Dear Lord God
the One
the Almighty
and Merciful

I think of the dead
who are living,
though we don't know.

I think of the living,
Dear Lord God,
who'd die
if they found out...

VIII

Is there another world
than this, the only one I know

Is there another Revelation
than this, the only one I hear

And is there another death,
Dear Lord God,
than this, the one I stare at

night after night after night…

IX

When we leave, oh God,
or when we return,
count us
just the same –

so the dead know that they've died.

CHRIS AGEE

FROM A Week in Sarajevo (1996)

The Bus Ride

I had flown to Split, but there was only one easy way onto Sarajevo if you were not IFOR, a UN official, a diplomat or some other member of the caravanserai of international agencies: the bus. Its route followed the coast to Ploce at the mouth of the Neretva, turning inland; crossed into the rich Herzegovinian plains at Metković; followed the river to Mostar and into the rugged Bosnian highlands; and, skirting Mount Igman, entered the swallow-shaped alpine valley which Sarajevo largely filled. In theory it would take eight hours, barring excessive delays by whatever the aftermath of four years of conflagration in BiH might cast up. It had, needless to say, only been operating since the oneset of the Dayton Accords three months earlier.

The Adriatic littoral of Istria and Dalmatia, with its thousand-plus islands, is where the Slav world embraces the warm oceans of the globe. Here there is that mingling of the Latin and the South Slavic which, further north round Trieste and its Slovene hinterland, so delighted Joyce. It is as if the template of an Italianate Mediterranean had been flecked with the East. Many of the beautiful towns of the region such as Split and Dubrovnik were founded by the Romans and owe much of their charm to the long hegemony of the Venetian Republic. As the road wove along the thin coastal incline that is southern Dalmatia, with its Slav signs and placenames, I kept feeling echoes from a dreamy concoction: Russia in the Mediterranean sun!

Dalmatia is Janus-faced geographically too: sea coast and mountain lie in close proximity. A great karst bulwark looms along the whole length of the littoral, separating the region from a desolate hinterland stretching to Herzegovina. The coast road's necklace – of pantiled houses, white walls, campaniles, vines, citrus, pine groves, arbors, balconies, a classic evergreen-scrub landscape rising precipitously towards grey peaks – had been unscathed by the war. At each high bend there appeared in the hazy light a new vista of sealine, coast-hugging island and barren limestone veined with snow. On headlands or outcrops, towns jewelled the pearly-blue clarity of a glittering Adriatic. Beautiful launches, all wood and naval white, were mirrored in harbours. Those two leitmotifs of Latin life, the café-bar, the house encircled by cultivation, were everywhere in evidence. It was March and already the first flush of blossom and bud was in train. The war was no more than distant thunder in a far range. Things had fallen apart beyond some cultural faultline or fire-break we had yet to cross.

It came, of course, in Herzegovina, not long after the trashy bor-der crossing at Metković.

The highlands of Herzegovina, wrote Hubert Butler sixty years ago, 'must be one of the most barren and desolate districts of Europe'. I got the first foretaste of this barrenness, rifted by fertility, even before reaching the border, when we turned into the foothills near Ploce. The road was winding and steep, and we rose into a terrain of extra-ordinary rockiness, a kind of low Adriatic sierra, more limestone crag and boulder than greenery. Only the occasional poplar-like cypress studded the half-lunar landscape like a slender minaret or the head of a paintbrush. Nestled in several valleys were small lakes of a dazzling, greyish, ultramarine clarity, the like of which I had never seen in freshwater.

Then, just as swiftly, we were descending towards the fertile delta flatlands of the Neretva, with its strip fields of fruit-trees, vines, olives, maize and great swathes of reeds. There was the same Mediterranean ambience as the coast, though with a more bland 'plains' inflection; but the little riverbank towns had a ramshackle, post-communist, industrial air. It was this anabasis of Mediterranean river plains into limestone ruggedness that our route followed, from the Dalmatian hills as far as the mountains of central Bosnia.

As the bus pulled out of Croatian customs, I waited for the unknown. In the first town I saw only two ruined houses. Ethnic-cleansing? Then, in the next town a few miles on, Klepci I believe, close to Medugorje, it started suddenly, ruination upon ruination; one half the town mostly destroyed, "building" to a kind of crescendo in certain places. Pocked; rubble-strewn; burnt and scorched; collapsed; littered with household goods and skeletons of vehicles; open-to-the-wind; masonry cratered and shattered; concrete tumuli; looted pre-mises; confetti of goods, glass, tiles, papers. A great frozen detritus of warring moments – the flash fireball of hatred. I was utterly gob-smacked by the juxtaposition of the unscathed and the annihilated.

Stalin once remarked that one is death is a tragedy, but a million is a statistic. Here the statistical had transmogrified in the other direction. Each ruin was a history, a scene of *tristia*, a tragedy with a veil of distance drawn between now and then. It was evident that the southernmost rim of the country's Muslims had been erased. It was as if an ethnic tornado had struck, wrecking here, sparing there; yet possessed of a kind of topsy-turvy order, a strangely coherent chaos. Apparently there had been two modes of assault on buildings, possibly denoting two stages of ethnic cleansing: a purposeful dynamiting from within (the "house" now a heap of masonry); and a simple torching and gutting without explosives. But however it was done, it was the HVO (the Bosnian Croat militia) that did it: their slogans were daubed on the ruins, like the red crosses of medieval vengeance mentioned by Marx.

The war between the Croat militia and the Bosnian Government in 1993-94 was partially ignited, then massively fuelled, by the partitionist maps drawn up by Lord Owen on behalf of the Foreign Ministers of the European Union. These conceded most of Herzegovina to a Croat mini-state; once they were in circulation, the clearing of vulnerable Muslims swept through the whole region south of Mostar. The extent to which this had been a scorched earth clearance was astounding. At places, not simply buildings but everything was burnt: pine groves, vineyards, graveyards, glasshouses. Already the ruins, like those of deserted Irish villages, were vanishing into overgrowth; becoming ghost places whose rawness of blood and pillage had faded.

As mile after mile of conflagration sailed past, Herzegovina came to seem a true wasteland. The bleakness was amplified by the greyness of unleafed spring (which also allowed a clear view of the ruins), the limestone crags, the hazy or leaden skies, the natural blowdown of fall and winter. Yet the victors' side had done it to themselves, too: the remaining inhabitants now had to live in a ravaged landscape, with the whole fabric of economy and culture laid waste.

Mostar was melancholy: a splendid city in ruins, like postwar Leningrad or Warsaw. We entered Muslim East Mostar, whose exquisite Ottoman riverside urbs had taken the brunt of devastation entailed by the battle between the banks. Everywhere antique Oriental buildings were gutted; indeed, the entire city centre had the air of an archaeological dig. One beautiful mosque had survived, but another was half-wrecked. The long roadside graveyard, with its bouquets and wooden markers in the shape of coffin-lids, was a great splash of colour in the spring dreariness. A number of civic edifices, including its own headquarters, had been renovated by the EU Administration, and a new concrete structure was replacing that gem of all Balkan bridges, which had given the city its name.

Not far past Mostar, the landscape began to rise and snow-clad mountains appeared in the distance. The river plains and Mediterranean architecture fell away, and we entered a great grey ascent of limestone gorges, crags, pillars, overlooks, escarpments. It became clear how the Bosnian heartland had defended itself: it simply lifted its

natural drawbridge by dynamiting the bridges which spanned the
dammed defiles.

Past this terrain of rock and further rock, the highland valleys were
lusher and more pastoral; there were hill-fields, orchards, woodpiles,
and lovely haystacks tipped with poles uncannily reminiscent of
Islamic domes. The road passed though several tunnels, and for a
while, as if a train enthusiast's fantasia, shadowed a railway. An
unfinished flyover ended in mid-air. It all put me in mind of a kind
of alpine version of the Appalachian roll of stream, hollow, gorge
and mountain: thickly forested with birch and evergreen, and gouged
by the Neretva's dazzling ultramarine clarity.

Outside beautiful Jablanice, the bus stopped for lunch at a road-
side café overlooking the town. There would be more war ahead, but
here at least was one unscathed vision of what the country had been.
Orchards and terraces ran from the back of houses right to the edge
of the deep river gorge, which split the town. With their pitched roofs,
overhanging eaves and high balconies, the houses too had an alpine
air. The white needle of a mosque rose from the clustered hillside. I
looked down at bungalow on the gorge's slope and saw a woman in
the pantaloons typical of country districts like Srebrenica. In the café,
a bubbling tank of highland trout was next to the twirling cartwheel
of a roasting lamb. We had crossed another faultline.

The Muezzin

'This,' said Vojka, 'is my favourite place in Sarajevo.' We were stand-
ing in a narrow cobblestoned street in the Baščaršija, the ancient
bazaar at the heart of the old Ottoman city. On one side, in a walled
courtyard with a covered fountain, was the great white double-domed
mosque of Gazi Husrevbeg, dating from the early 16th century:
Bosnia's largest, and one of the most beautiful in the Balkans. On the
other side, beyond a low wall and arched gate, there was the small
Gazi Husrevbeg medresa or theological school, of similar antiquity,
with its pitched metallic roof and eight chimneys, one of only two
surviving to modern times. Both were founded by their namesake,
and both, following Seljuk building tradition, have scalloped portals
of a verdigris hue, adorned with stalactites and Arabic calligraphy.
All around are the wood-fronted low-eaved shopfronts of the quar-
ter, framed by their street benches and tiled bays. The whole area
was relentlessly targeted by the Serbs – and as relentlessly rebuilt
by the shopowners right through the siege.

I had wanted to see three o'clock prayers and we approached the Islamic equivalent of a verger, blue-coated, in the courtyard. He looked dubiously at us from under his black beret, but then shrugged me in, calling to Vojka when I stepped on the mat under the portico without removing my shoes. Inside was filled entirely, from dome to floor, with several tiers of scaffolding. The domes and svelte minaret had taken several dozen hits, and a full-scale restoration was planned, funded by overseas Muslims. I could just discern some ancient arabesque design on the flaking, whitish walls. Light came from the large dome's row of Arab arches. A single prayer-line was assembling before the ghost of an alcove adorned again with scalloped stalactites and gold calligraphy.

I felt as if I was in the presence of some rich taproot, some vein of antiquity, the very Chartres of an alpine Islam. I sat down, cross-legged, at the back amidst the scaffolding. The floor was a soft sea of kelims dotted with prayer beads. I loved the spartan simplicity, the form and void, the stone and light, the meaning in space. The feeling as well of a tradition whose patina of suppleness had remained intact, unburnished by self-consciousness, by the modern cults of the revived, the literal, the authentic. Not for the first time, I wondered at a temperamental affinity between Islam, Buddhism and the plain Protestantism of, say, the Shakers. And I felt too, if did not actually recall, the words of Danilo Kiš: 'Bosnia, that exotic land at the heart of Europe…'

Twenty or so men had gathered, including a young soldier. The imam in his robe and maroon-and-cream turban entered, and prayers began: now upright and open-palmed, now kneeling and prostrate. Suddenly, from an eyrie in the scaffolding I hadn't noticed, the muezzin began singing. Voice filled the vault, beseeched the Void, plangent and guttural: the plainsong of Islam, a sort of sacral sean-nós, invoking Allah.

All of it, of course, as European as a rose-window or cantor before the ark. What rough beast had possessed the gunners in the hills? As prayers broke up, the soldier shot me a disapproving glance. I agreed: he was entitled to his animosity.

After all, more than a thousand mosques, half Bosnia's total, have been razed. Untold numbers of other Ottoman treasures, the most tangible expression of the Muslim strand of Bosnia's polyphonic heritage – mesdžids (small, often wooden mosques without minarets), dervish houses for meditation, mausoleums and headstones, bridges, bazaars, wells, fountains, baths, bridges, whole urban environments of extraordinary beauty – have been extinguished forever. In most of northern and eastern Bosnia, then, not only the presence of Muslims

but their communal memories – records, monuments, creative works,
fruits of the heart preserved in books or expressed in stone – have
been systematically extirpated. Sitting there as the mosque emptied,
I remembered the gist of the Mufti of Sarajevo's plea to the outside
world: 'We call upon all Muslim clerics in the name of Muslim
Altruism, on the leadership of all the Christian denominations –
Catholic, Orthodox, Protestant – in the name of Christian love and
mercy, on the Jewish Rabbinate in the name of supreme justice, and
on every Buddhist in the name of Buddha's compassion, as well as
secular humanists in the name of their principles, to help us...'
    What rough beast, indeed, had possessed the élites of the West,
mesmerised by the horror, standing idly by whilst denying the victims
a means of defence? Something of the soldier's feeling still reddens
and darkens my own mind whenever I think of that collective
Chamberlain, including our own supine Tánaiste, that for so long
has haunted the Chancelleries of the European Union. Not here, but
in the councils of civilised Europe, the post-war mantra of *never
again!* was rendered hollow guff.

At Edo's Studio

One dusk I joined two painters, the Swede Jan Hafström and the
Bosnian Edo Numankadić, to visit the latter's atelier. Somehow, the
three of us got to know another in a series of interludes, intersections
really, snatched from our hectic and occasionally parallel routes
across the last week of the Festival. Edo's studio was in the distant
suburbs, part of the New Sarajevo that had mushroomed into the wider
valley after the Second World War. One of six atop a residential
towerblock near the old front lines, it was the last still occupied.
    Spartan, poor even, before the war, life in this suburb was now
truly bleak. In the first months of the siege a single JNA tank had
blasted away at the district, its massive towers on open ground easy
targets. A huge bomb, painstakingly fashioned from an air-rocket,
had towards the end of the war taken out the corner of three floors of
the adjacent building. Edo pointed out the place on the pavement,
before the block, marked by a surprisingly small mortar-splash which
'commemorated' the murder of seven little children and their teacher
in the creche which it devastated.
    Edo's studio was full of tranquil and harmonious studies of colour
and form, reminding me both of kelims and Rothko. As we sat sipping
Turkish coffee, and as Edo spoke of the role of culture during the

war and in its aftermath – how for many it was a lifeline more precious than bread, how important it was for outsiders to come – the plangent chant of the muezzin wafted up from the makeshift mosque where the creche had been. The barricaded window was slung open, and we looked out on this sad, haunting and noble city: out over the small siege gardens, the trenches, the suburbs like shooting galleries stretching to Mount Igman in the mist. 'Where are we after all,' Jan said later, 'if not the place our tools have prepared us for?'

True moment of *tristia!* Each of us had felt it, detained there in silence, and the next hour round the coffee-table seemed defined by its epiphany. Edo described the atmosphere of Sarajevo cultural life in the late sixties and seventies, with its longing for a cosmopolitan "spirit of the times", beyond the provincial if benign confines of Yugoslav Communism.

He knew Karadžić then, and remembered him well: long hair; long leather jacket and platform shoes; a Montenegrin with grandiose illusions about being a great poet (for the greatest Montenegrins have been poets). In short, the kind of person people avoided. He had also been a notorious gambler; and so had probably been enlisted by Belgrade due to some perception of the suitability of his temperament. As Edo went off to a table in search of some new work, Jan and I remarked on how forcefully in Sarajevo you were reminded of the rich experience of listening *everywhere*: everyone here had a siege-history, a fund of stories, which you glimpsed as if the edge of a veil had been lifted. Fittingly, as we rose, I noticed, on the wall by the door, a poster for a group exhibition during the war: *Witness to Existence.*

Leaving, the three of us jogging down the stairs, I was suddenly struck by the sheer mystery of it all: the dusky tiled chipped stairwell; the death; the light in opaque glass; this place and moment, being here, all our feelings...

Out in the fresh air the far-facing hills glimmered like a starry sky. The makeshift mosque was emptying, a few older men in skullcaps heading home. We passed again the sadness of mortar-splashes.

The only time Edo had ever cried during the war was when he was abroad. He had been watching a woman who had been moved by some photographs of the city. It was as if he was seeing innocence. It reminded him of that father on the news who had held his daughter with her shattered arm and said he would just like to sit down over coffee and ask the Chetnik why he had done it.

Two Purchases

Of course I had left gift-buying to the last moment. Vojka and I got to the Baščaršija round six, just as the first small bazaar windows began to darken. We raced from shop to shop, and I scanned quickly the copperwork, slippers, silver filigree jewellery and Balkan coffee pots that were that were their stock-in-trade. Nothing much caught my eye. So Vojka suggested we try the more bohemian shop we had paused in during an earlier walk-about, one that specialised in the antiques and paintings which the siege had forced onto the market.

I noticed at once a small impressionistic head of a lady in a broad hat fastened round her chin with a sash. Could it be one of Affan's? Sure enough, there was a faint signature scratched in the paint, and Vojka judged it at once an early work. I haggled for a short while and bought it for a song in deutchmarks, the reigning currency. We stepped out into the late brightness of dusk and passed where at midday I had had my first burek – warm, delicious, messy. Somehow I had not wanted to shift from that bench, and just idled there, for the first time in a week, soaking up the sunshine and watching an old lady in leggings, greatcoat and boots eat ravenously, then limp off like Mother Courage. In the language of things, the battered vista before me, with its planes and sunny wasteground, seemed to whisper *chance* and *survival*.

The purchase exhilarated us. 'Now you will have a real gift from Sarajevo.' We entered the lane between Gazi Husrevbeg Mosque and its medresa. The streets of the Baščaršija were crowded with a Heraclitean flow of evening walkers, tramping past the sites of agony ghosted with shrapnel-marks, like the bread queue's splash I passed each morning. How long would remembrance be keen, now that repairs had begun and the bright lights of commerce were shafting the gloom of aftermath? Life, of course, loves to forget.

I had now walked here many times and, looking ahead, once again called to mind Francis Jones' words about this being the city's still centre, the very essence of Islam: 'a walled courtyard, water, a tree, and the warm geometry of stone. In the deep blue velvet sky by the minaret hung a sliver of incandescent silver light...'

Something there is in reality that needs to be spoken to be felt. Vojka slowed and gripped my elbow. There, in the pellucid air, risen above the lime and the minaret with its conical green cap, was the month's new crescent, waxing towards plenitude.